Garfield's

Party Time
Favorites

by
Margaret Garfield

Garfield's Party Time Favorites

by
Margaret Garfield

First Printing — August, 1985
Copyright © 1985 by
Garfield's Party Time Favorites Publishing
Site #35-6, R.R.#1
Okanagan Falls, B.C.
Canada   V0H 1R0

Canadian Cataloguing in Publication Data
Garfield, Margaret
  Garfield's party time favorites

Includes index.
ISBN 0-919845-29-0

1. Alcoholic beverages. 2. Beverages. I. Title.
TX815.G37 1985   641.8'7   C85-091430-2

Photography by
Patricia Holdsworth
Patricia Holdsworth Photography
Regina, Saskatchewan

Designed, Printed and Produced in Canada by
Centax of Canada
Publishing Consultant: Margo Embury
Design by: Blair Fraser
1048 Fleury Street
Regina, Saskatchewan, Canada S4N 4W8
(306) 359-3737

#105 - 4711 13 Street N.E.
Calgary, Alberta, Canada   T2E 6M3

TABLE OF CONTENTS

PARTY-TIME FAVORITES

The art of making your favorite drinks is truly creative, inexpensive, a lot of fun and becoming more and more popular all the time. Most of the equipment is found right in your kitchen, while recipe ingredients can be found in your local wine shops.

Over the years I have collected, compiled and created my own drinks. One day I had a great idea. "Why not write a book so that others may enjoy them also." So here it is, I'm sure you will enjoy using the book as much as I have enjoyed putting it together.

A very special thanks to all those people who so generously contributed their time and recipes in order to make this book possible.

Margaret E. Garfield

Margaret Garfield

WINES

The art of making wine dates back to prehistoric man. No one really knows who the first winemakers were. Wine had a more practical reason in its beginning than the mere pleasure of drinking. Ancient peoples had little pure water to drink and they learned that alcohol formed by fermentation protected fruit juice from spoiling. People who drank this fermented juice did not get sick as often as those who drank the impure water. For medicinal values as well as cooking and pure pleasure, wine making and drinking continues today in a very large and sophisticated way.

The chief grape growing areas in Canada are the Niagara Peninsula of Ontario and the Okanagan Valley of British Columbia. There are more than 28,000 acres yielding more than 90,000 tons annually.

Some wines in Canada are made from imported grapes or juice, while others may be a blend of Canadian and imported grapes. Blending is an art requiring great skill and knowledge by the wine industry.

Because of its sugar content fruit juice ferments very easily. Fermentation takes place almost immediately after the fruit is crushed, however some fruit may require additional sugar. The most widely used fruits for wine are the grape, cherry, blackberry, blueberry, raspberry, loganberry and apple.

Wine is a natural beverage that has been enjoyed for thousands of years. You don't have to be an expert to enjoy a good glass of wine, whether it be light, red, white, champagne, crackling, aperitif or dessert wine. There are wines for every occasion.

Wine Varieties

Appetizer wines or aperitifs

Are wines served before a meal to stimulate the appetite. Some of the wines used are white, champagne, sherry and vermouths. However there is a wide variety of light wines which may be used. Serve at room temperature or lightly chilled.

Table wines

Have an alcoholic content of 14% or less. They come in white, red or rosé. Burgundy, Bordeaux, Claret, Moselle, Tokay, Rhine, Chablis and Sauternes are just a few of the light table wines. They may be sweet, medium-dry or dry. Table wines once opened should be refrigerated and used within a few days because of the low sugar content.

White table wines should be served lightly chilled.

Red wine likes to breathe and will benefit if opened and exposed to the air for about 20 minutes before serving. Red wines are usually served at room temperature.

Rosé table wines are light, all-purpose wines which can be served with most foods at any time. They come in medium-sweet and dry and should be well chilled before serving.

Fortified wines or dessert wines

Are those whose alcohol content has been increased to as much as 21% in volume by the addition of brandy or other spirits. Among these wines are port, muscatel, sherry, Tokay, Madeira, kosher wines and fruit wines. They can be either sweet or dry.

Sparkling wines

Are light wines that bubble and fizz when they are poured because of carbon dioxide. They have less than 7% alcohol content. The sparkling wines include champagne, sparkling burgundy, sparkling Rhine, sparkling Moselle to name a few. Bubbly wines should be well chilled before serving.

Crackling wines

Petillant as they are sometimes referred to, have a mild effervescence and come in red, rosé or white. The alcohol content may run 14% by volume and they are less bubbly than sparkling wine.

Wine Varieties

Aromatized wines
Include Dubonnet and French and Italian vermouths. Such wines have an alcohol content of 15-20% and contain wormwood and other aromatic herbs and spices.

Vintage wine
Is wine labelled with the year most of the grapes were harvested and made into wine. This generally refers to an exceptionally good year.

Serving Wine

Wine
Should be served in clear, stemmed glasses which range in size from a small glass for port to the fluted or tulip glass for champagne.
It is most important to hold a wine glass by the stem to prevent the heat of your hand from altering the temperture of the wine.

White wine
Should be served in an elongated U-shaped glass narrower at the top to prevent bubbles from dissipating.

Dessert and appetizer wine glasses:
3-4 oz. Fill glasses ⅔ full.

Champagne glass:
7-8 oz. fluted or tulip glass. Fill ⅔ full. Never use the saucer-shaped champagne glass as the precious bubbles are lost almost immediately after serving. "What is Champagne without the bubbles"?

An all-purpose glass:
6-8 oz. Fill ⅔ full when serving wines. However fill only ½ full when serving appetizer or dessert wines.

Serving Wine

What is the proper wine to serve with:
Appetizer or soup — dry sherry
Oysters or fish — dry white wine
Red meat — dry red wine
Creamed dishes — dry white wine
Fowl — dry white wine
Wild game — burgundy
Dessert — sparkling or sweet wine

All wines have a number which indicates the degree of sweetness of the wine, which are as follows:
0 — very dry
1- 2 — dry
3- 4 — medium
5- 6 — sweet
7-10 — very sweet

In some areas the number classification goes to 20 but 0 is always very dry with the high number being very sweet.

Brut
The driest of champagne or sparkling wines.

Mouseux
Another word for sparkling wine.

Petillant
Light sparkling.

Extra dry
Slightly sweet (a term used on champagne labels).

Sec
French word for dry.

Secco
Italian word for dry.

Sekt
German sparkling wines.

SPIRITS

"Spirits": A word used to identify alcoholic beverages containing ethyl alcohol. The amount of alcohol may be as little as 2% as in some beers, or it may be as much as 68% as in absinthe. The alcohol content of some beverages is measured in proof which is about twice the percentage of alcohol by volume. The alcohol in these drinks is obtained by fermenting sugar or such starchy products as corn, barley, wheat, rye, rice, and potatoes, to change their starch into sugar. Beverage alcohol may also be obtained by distilling fermented mashed fruit.

Brandy

Is obtained by distilling wine or a fermented fruit mash, after it has been aged in wooden casks. The alcoholic content of brandy is 45-55%. The brandies include cognac, Armagnac, applejack, kirsch and other fruit brandies.

Gin

Is made by distilling mash or rye, corn or other grain in a special kind of still called a "pot still". It can also be made by adding essential oils to alcohol. Gin contains about 40% alcohol. Juniper berries give gin its flavor. It is usually not aged.

Rum

Is distilled from sugar cane or molasses fermented.

Vodka

Is a Russian beverage distilled from potatoes or a fermented mash of rye, barley and corn. Vodka is not flavored and has no taste of its own.

Whiskey

Is distilled from a fermented mash of corn, rye, barley or wheat. It is then aged in wooden barrels. Whiskeys have an alcoholic content ranging 40-50%. **Irish whiskey** is made from from malt, barley and other grains while **Scotch whiskey** is made primarily from barley and **Bourbon whiskey** was originally produced from corn.

LIQUEURS

Absinthe — a licorice-flavored cordial. Made from brandy, wormwood and other herbs. It has been taken off the market and replaced with anisette and Pernod.

Amer Picon — cordial, orange-flavored and bitter (French aperitif).

Applejack — American term for apple brandy.

Aquavit — potato-based liqueur from Scandinavia flavored with caraway seeds.

Benedictine — cordial made from herbs.

Bitters — made from roots, barks, herbs and berries. Aromatic and bitter taste. Angostura bitters, Abbott's bitters and orange bitters.

Byrrh — French apertif.

Calvados — apple brandy from France.

Campari — Italian aperitif.

Chartreuse — cordial, comes in green or yellow according to the flavorings used. These include palm leaves, peppermint, orange peel and spices.

Cherry Heering — cherry-flavored liqueur.

Cointreau — orange-flavored liqueur.

Compounded Liquors — are pure distilled spirits that have been flavored with various seeds, roots and leaves.

Cordial or Liqueur — is made by combining some spirit, such as brandy with sugar and certain flavorings, such as the various fruits.

Plant Cordials — include crème de menthe, crème de cacao and crème de rose.

Cordial Médoc — chocolate-flavored French liqueur. Dark red in color.

Crème de Cacao — chocolate-flavored liqueur.

Crème de Cassis — blackcurrant liqueur.

Crème de Menthe — peppermint-flavored liqueur, green or white in color.

Crème de Moyaux — brandy-based liqueur with apricot and peach flavor.

Curaçao Liqueur — flavored with the dried peel of the bitter oranges, caraway seeds and anise-flavored kummel.

10

LIQUEURS

Drambuie — Scotch whiskey-based liqueur from Scotland.

Dubonnet — French aperitif.

Fino Sherry — pale dry sherry.

Grand Marnier — orange-flavored liqueur.

Grenadine — pomegranate-flavored syrup.

Kirsch — (or Kirschwasser) Colorless cherry brandy.

Kümmel — German liqueur flavored with aniseed and cumin.

Lillet — French apertif.

Madeira — fortified wine from Madeira.

Maraschino Liqueur — made from sour cherries and honey. White in color and used as a flavoring agent.

Marsala — Italian dessert wine.

Orgeat — almond-flavored liqueur.

Pernod — aniseed-flavored aperitif.

Pisco Brandy — Peruvian brandy.

Prunelle — blackthorn (sloe)-flavored liqueur.

Sake — Japanese rice wine, has an alcoholic content of 14 to 16% by volume.

Slivovitz — plum brandy.

Sloe gin — is not a true gin, but a liqueur flavored with sloe (blackthorn).

Southern Comfort — brandy-and-bourbon-based American liqueur.

Strega — Italian liqueur.

Tequila — Mexico's most popular drink, is made from the juice of the agave plant.

Triple Sec — orange-flavored liqueur.

BARTENDING TIPS

Ice
Crushed or shaved ice is best for frappés and other tall drinks for sipping through straws.
Cracked or cubed ice is best for stirring and shaking drinks.

For decorative ice
Place maraschino cherry in each ice cube tray and fill with water to freeze. Put 1 cube in each glass when serving drinks.

Decorative ice ring or mold
Fill a ring or mold ¼ full with water, partially freeze. Add fruit of your choice, citrus slices, pineapple chunks, maraschino cherries or fruit in season. Arrange in decorative design. Freeze to anchor fruit, fill with ice water and freeze until firm.

Mixing Drinks
Mix drinks in order given. Usually syrup or sugar, ice, liquor, and when ready to serve, carbonated beverages.
Stir drinks containing carbonated mixer very gently.
Do not stir liqueurs.
Shaking and Blending is very important in drinks where fruit juices, sugar, eggs, and cream are used. Use a blender if available, or shake very well.

Garnishes
Twists of peel should have all white removed from peel. Rub skin of peel around the rim of glass to coat it with its natural oil.
Add oil from peel to drink by twisting over the glass then drop into glass.
Slices should be slit up to the center to saddle rim of glass.
Olives should be washed before using in drinks
To sugarfrost, wet the rim of a chilled glass with lime or lemon, then dip into powdered sugar.

BARTENDING TIPS

Pousse-café or shooter
Is made from several liqueurs poured very gently over the back of a spoon into a glass so that one floats atop another. Each has a different weight and must be poured in the order given, from the heaviest to the lightest which permits floating. Do not stir.

Vanilla bean
may be dried and used again.

To flame liquor
Preheat 1 spoon of liquor over a flame and set afire. Carefully pour flaming liquor into remaining beverage.

Sugar syrups
Depending on sweetness, can be made by dissolving 2 parts sugar to 1 part water, or for sweeter syrup 3 parts sugar to 1 part water, less sweet 1 cup sugar to 1 cup water. Refrigerate.

To keep eggnog cool
Place the filled punch bowl in a larger bowl filled with ice. Or freeze some of the eggnog into cubes or a mold and add to the punch when serving. It will keep it chilled but won't dilute the eggnog.

MEASUREMENTS

1 pony	= 1 oz.
1 jigger	= 1½ oz. or 3 tbsp.
1 tsp.	= ⅛ oz.
1 dash	= 4-5 drops
1 bar-spoon	= ½ tsp.
1 tbsp.	= ½ oz.
24 drops	= ¼ tsp.
3 tsp.	= 1 tbsp.
2 tbsp.	= 1 fluid oz.
16 tbsp.	= 1 cup
1 fifth	= 25.6 oz.
tsp.	= teaspoon
tbsp.	= tablespoon
lb.	= pound
oz.	= ounce

METRIC

2 mL	= ½ tsp.
5 mL	= 1 tsp.
7 mL	= 1½ tsp.
15 mL	= 1 tbsp.
25 mL	= 1 coffee spoon
30 mL	= 1 fluid oz.
50 mL	= ¼ cup
60 mL	= 1 small sherry glass
75 mL	= ⅓ cup
125 mL	= ½ cup or 4 oz.
187 mL	= 6.6 oz.
250 mL	= 1 generous cup = 8 oz.
300 mL	= 1 can sweetened condensed milk
375 mL	= 13.2 oz.
385 mL	= 1 can evaporated milk
500 mL	= 17.6 oz.
750 mL	= 26.4 oz.
960 mL	= 32 oz. = 4 cups
1.0 litre	= 35.2 oz.
225 gram (weight)	= 8 oz.
450 gram (weight)	= 16 oz.

BAR TOOLS

ice bucket

tongs

lemon/lime
juicer

blender

shaker with spout
and strainer

pitcher

corkscrew

wire strainer

muddler

double-ended
jigger
pony — 1 oz.
jigger — 1.5 oz.

15

GLASSES

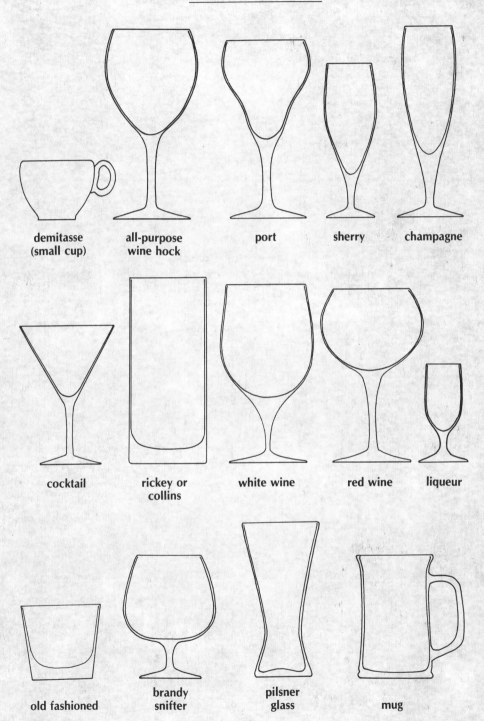

demitasse (small cup)

all-purpose wine hock

port

sherry

champagne

cocktail

rickey or collins

white wine

red wine

liqueur

old fashioned

brandy snifter

pilsner glass

mug

ALFONSO SPECIAL

¾ oz.	dry gin	20 mL
1½ oz.	Grand Marnier	45 mL
few drops	each sweet vermouth and dry vermouth	few drops
few dashes	Angostura bitters	few dashes

Combine with ice; shake. Strain and add ice.

AMERICAN BEAUTY

¼ oz.	crème de menthe	8 mL
½ oz.	brandy	15 mL
½ oz.	dry vermouth	15 mL
¼ oz.	grenadine	8 mL
¾ oz.	port	20 mL
½ oz.	orange juice	15 mL

Combine with ice; shake well. Strain carefully, then add the port, tipping the glass so that the port floats on top.

AUNT JEMIMA

1½ oz.	brandy	45 mL
1½ oz.	crème de cacao	45 mL
1½ oz.	Benedictine	45 mL

Combine, carefully tilting the glass so that each ingredient floats upon the other.

BACARDI COCKTAIL

2 jiggers	Bacardi rum	90 mL
	juice of ½ lime	
2 dashes	sugar syrup	

Shake well with ice and strain into glass.

BACARDI AND OJ

1½ oz.	Bacardi rum	45 mL
	orange juice, ice cold	
	lemon or lime wedge	

Pour rum over ice. Add juice and a squeeze of lemon.

BACARDI DAIQUIRI

	juice of ½ a lime or lemon	
½ tsp.	sugar	2 mL
1½ oz.	rum	45 mL

Shake together with crushed ice. Strain and serve.

BANANA SLUSH

5	bananas	5
12½ oz.	frozen lemon concentrate	355 mL
12½ oz.	frozen orange concentrate	355 mL
48 oz.	unsweetened pineapple juice	1.36 L
26 oz.	liquor of your choice	750 mL

Combine in blender, then freeze. Serve with 7-Up or Sprite.

BANSHEE

1 oz.	white crème de cacao	30 mL
1 oz.	crème de banana	30 mL
1 oz.	light cream	30 mL

Combine with ice; shake very well. Strain. Serve.

BENEDICTINE COCKTAIL

3 oz.	Benedictine	90 mL
½	lemon	½
few dashes	Angostura bitters	few dashes
	powdered sugar	

Combine Benedictine with bitters. Shake only a few seconds. Rub the lemon around the rim of a glass and press the rim in powdered sugar. Add a cherry, Benedictine and ice.

BETWEEN THE SHEETS

1 oz.	brandy	30 mL
1 oz.	Cointreau	30 mL
1 oz.	light rum	30 mL

Combine with ice. Shake well. Strain and add ice.

BLACKCURRANT SLUSH

1 oz.	crème de cassis	30 mL
	(blackcurrant liqueur)	
1 oz.	pineapple juice	30 mL
2 tsp.	brandy	10 mL

Combine the ingredients in an electric blender. Add 3 oz. of crushed ice, and blend at low speed for no more than 15 seconds. Strain the drink into a wide champagne glass and serve or freeze.

BLACK RUSSIAN

| 1½ oz. | vodka | 45 mL |
| ¾ oz. | Kahlúa | 20 mL |

Combine with ice; shake well. Strain and add ice. Serve in old fashioned glass.

See photograph page 16.

BLOODY MARY

	ice	
6 dashes	Worcestershire sauce	6 dashes
3 dashes	of Tabasco	3 dashes
	pinch of salt and pepper	
	juice of ½ lemon	
2 jiggers	vodka	90 mL
	tomato juice	

Put first 6 ingredients in a glass. Fill remainder of glass with tomato juice. No celery.

BLUEBERRY TEA

	Grand Marnier	30 mL
1 oz.	hot tea	1 mug
1 mug		

Combine.

BOBSLEIGH

1 jigger	orange liqueur	45 mL
2 jiggers	vodka	90 mL

Half fill a tumbler with crushed ice. Pour in orange liqueur and vodka. Garnish with full orange slice and drop in a maraschino cherry.

BRANDY ALEXANDER

1 jigger	brandy	45 mL
½ jigger	crème de cacao	20 mL
½ jigger	heavy cream	20 mL

Combine with ice; shake well. Strain and serve in chilled cocktail glass. Sprinkle with nutmeg.

Also: Gin and Rum Alexander, or substitute Kahlúa for the dark crème de cacao.

BROWN COW

| 1½ oz. | Kahlúa | 45 mL |
| | cream to fill | |

Serve over ice in old fashioned glass.

BULL SHOT

1 dash	Worcestershire sauce	1 dash
4 oz.	cold beef bouillon	125 mL
1½ oz.	vodka	45 mL

Pour over ice in old fashioned glass. Add lemon twist.

CAESAR

	celery salt	
1 dash	Tabasco	1 dash
2 dashes	Worcestershire sauce	2 dashes
	salt and pepper to taste	
2 oz.	vodka	60 mL
4-6 oz.	Clamato juice	125-175 mL

Rim glass with celery salt. Add ice cubes, then rest of ingredients. Garnish with celery stick and slice of lime.
See photograph on cover.

CARIBBEAN COCKTAIL

2 oz.	white rum	60 mL
8 oz.	pineapple juice	250 mL
2 tbsp.	lime juice	25 mL
1 oz.	sugar syrup	30 mL
1-2 dashes	orange bitters	1-2 dashes
	club soda	

Combine all but soda with ice; shake. Strain; add ice and soda.

CHAMPAGNE COCKTAIL

| 1 lump | sugar in champagne glass | 1 lump |
| 1 dash | Angostura bitters orange and lemon twists champagne | 1 dash |

Put bitters on sugar. Add twists, fill glass with champagne.

CHERYL'S SLUSH

12½ oz.	orange concentrate	355 mL
12½ oz.	pink lemonade concentrate	355 mL
26 oz.	vodka	750 mL
7 cups	water	1.75 L
½ cup	sugar	125 mL

Combine water and sugar and boil together until sugar is dissolved. Add all ingredients, stir and put in ice cream pail. Freeze 24 hours. Add Sprite or 7-Up to fill glasses when serving.

CHI CHI

1½ oz.	vodka	45 mL
¾ cup	pineapple	175 mL
2 oz.	coconut syrup	60 mL
2 oz.	cream	60 mL
1 cup	crushed ice	250 mL

Blend in blender. Garnish with pineapple and cherry.

CLARET COBBLER

½ tumbler	cracked ice	½ tumbler
1 dash	maraschino liqueur	1 dash
1 tsp.	each sugar, lemon juice claret	5 mL

Add maraschino and juice to ice. Fill with claret and garnish with fruit.

22

COFFEE COCKTAIL

1 oz.	brandy	30 mL
1 oz.	Cointreau	30 mL
1 oz.	cold black coffee	30 mL

Shake well with ice. Best for after-dinner drink.

COFFEE GRAND MARNIER

¾ oz.	Kahlúa	20 mL
¾ oz.	Grand Marnier	20 mL
1 tbsp.	orange juice	15 mL

Combine without ice; stir well. Pour over crushed ice. Top with an orange slice.

COFFEE KIRSCH

1 oz.	kirsch	30 mL
1	egg white	1
4 oz.	coffee	125 mL
pinch	sugar	pinch

Combine with ice; shake well. Strain and add ice.

COLLINS

1½ jiggers	rum, gin, vodka, or whisky	45 mL
	juice of 1 lemon	1
1 tsp.	powdered sugar	5 mL

Shake well with ice. Pour into glass, fill with soda water.

CUBA LIBRE

2-3	ice cubes	2-3
2 jiggers	rum	90 mL
	juice of ½ lemon	
	cola	

Place ice cubes in large highball glass and add rum, lemon juice and fill with cola. Stir and serve.
See photograph on cover.

DAIQUIRI

2 jiggers	light rum	90 mL
1 tbsp.	lime or lemon juice	15 mL
2 tsp.	powdered sugar	10 mL

Blend with 2 cups (500 mL) fine ice until like snow. Serve with a straw.
See photograph page 16.

EARTHQUAKE

1 oz.	whisky	30 mL
1 oz.	gin	30 mL
1 oz.	Pernod	30 mL

Shake well with ice. Pour into glass.

EL PRESIDENTE

1½ oz.	rum	45 mL
1 oz.	Curaçao	30 mL
1 oz.	dry vermouth	30 mL
dash	grenadine syrup	dash
	cracked ice	

Combine first 4 ingredients and pour over the ice.

ENGLISH SANGRIA

6	black currant tea bags	6
	OR	
½ cup	loose black currant tea	125 mL
2 cups	boiling water	500 mL
½ cup	sugar	125 mL
2 cups	tawny port wine	500 mL
2	oranges, thinly sliced	2
1	lime, thinly sliced	1
2 cups	club soda, chilled	500 mL
	ice cubes	

Pour boiling water over tea, steep for 5 minutes. Strain, and stir in sugar until dissolved. Chill. To serve, pour tea mixture into a 3-quart pitcher, stir in wine, fruit, soda and ice.

FRENCH "75"

1 oz.	vodka or gin	30 mL
1 tbsp.	lemon juice	15 mL
1 tsp.	superfine sugar	5 mL
	ice cubes	
	chilled champagne	
	lemon peel spiral	

Shake liquor, juice and sugar with ice; strain into 8-oz. (250 mL) glass. Fill with champagne, Garnish with peel.

FROSTED MINT COCOA

4 oz.	cocoa	125 mL
6 oz.	sugar	175 mL
1 cup	boiling water	250 mL
5 cups	milk	1.25 L
3 cups	vanilla ice cream	750 mL
3 oz.	white crème de menthe	90 mL

Combine cocoa and sugar with boiling water. Simmer for several minutes. Warm milk in a double boiler; add cocoa mixture and crème de menthe. Stir well, cool. Combine cocoa mixture with ice cream; blend until smooth.

FROZEN STEPPES

2 oz.	vanilla ice cream	60 mL
2 tbsp.	vodka	25 mL
1 tbsp.	dark crème de cacao	15 mL
3 oz.	cracked ice	90 mL

Combine in a blender at a high speed until smooth. Serve.

GIBSON

3 oz.	dry gin	90 mL
1 oz.	dry vermouth	30 mL

Stir with ice. Serve with pickled onion.

GILBERT AND SULLIVAN

1½ oz.	vodka	45 mL
3 oz.	sweet sherry	90 mL
2 dashes	bitters	2 dashes

Stir well, add ice.

GIMLET

2 oz.	English gin	60 mL
2 oz.	lime juice	60 mL

Stir gently, add ice cubes.

GIN AND TONIC

3	ice cubes	3
2 jiggers	gin	90 mL
½ slice	lemon	½ slice
	tonic water	

Place ice cubes in tall highball glass. Add gin, crush and add
½ slice lemon. Fill with tonic water.

GIN FIZZ

2 jiggers	dry gin	90 mL
1 tbsp.	powdered sugar	15 mL
	juice each ½ lemon and lime	
	club soda	

Combine gin, sugar, and juice with ice, shake well. Strain, add ice and fill with club soda.

GOLDEN CADILLAC

1 oz.	Galliano	30 mL
½ oz.	white cacao	15 mL
1 oz.	heavy cream	30 mL
3 oz.	crushed ice	90 mL

Combine in a blender at a low speed for 15 seconds. Strain and serve.

GOLDEN SLIPPER

¾ oz.	yellow Chartreuse	20 mL
¾ oz.	apricot brandy	20 mL
1	egg yolk	1

Combine with ice; shake well. Strain and add ice.

GRASSHOPPER

1½ oz.	crème de menthe	45 mL
1 oz.	crème de cacao	30 mL
1 oz.	heavy cream	30 mL

Mix with ice; shake well. Strain and serve.

HARVEY WALLBANGER

1 oz.	vodka	30 mL
	orange juice	
1 oz.	Galliano	30 mL

Pour vodka into highball glass. Add ice and almost fill the glass with orange juice. Float Galliano on top. Garnish with cherry and orange slice.

HAWAIIAN VODKA

1 oz.	pineapple juice	30 mL
	juice of 1 lemon	
	juice of 1 orange (or 4 tbsp. [60 mL] canned unsweetened)	
1 tsp.	grenadine	5 mL
2 oz.	vodka	60 mL

Shake until a frost forms. Pour into serving glass.

HAWAIIAN SLING

1 tbsp.	vodka	15 mL
1 oz.	sherry	30 mL
1 oz.	Hawaiian punch	30 mL

Combine with ice. Shake well. Strain. Serve over ice.

HURRICANE

1 oz.	dry gin	30 mL
1 oz.	whisky	30 mL
1 oz.	crème de menthe	30 mL
	juice of 2 lemons	

Combine with ice; shake. Strain add ice.

HURRICANE COOLER

1 oz.	white rum	30 mL
1 oz.	Jamaican rum	30 mL
1 oz.	lime juice	30 mL
1	pineapple stick	1
2 oz.	orange juice	60 mL
1 tbsp.	sugar syrup	15 mL
2 tsp.	orange bitters	10 mL
few drops	Pernod	few drops

Combine with ice; shake well. Strain over crushed ice. Garnish with the pineapple stick and cherry.

ICEBREAKER

1 oz.	white rum	30 mL
½ oz.	cherry brandy	15 mL

Put in old fashioned glass with crushed ice. Stir and serve with 2 small straws.

KAHLÚA COLADA

1½ oz.	Kahlúa	45 mL
1½ oz.	pineapple juice	45 mL
1 oz.	coconut cream	30 mL
1 cup	crushed ice	250 mL

Blend and pour into a tall glass.

KAHLÚA MINT

1 oz.	Kahlúa	30 mL
½ oz.	peppermint schnapps	15 mL
	soda water	

Combine over ice and top with soda to taste.

KING ALPHONSE

crème de cacao
heavy cream

Fill liqueur glass ¾ full with dark crème de cacao and float
¼ heavy cream on top and serve.

KIRNOFF

1 oz.	vodka	30 mL
1½ oz.	white wine	45 mL
½ oz.	crème de cassis	15 mL

Combine and serve chilled in stem glass.

KNOCK-OUT

1 oz.	gin	30 mL
1 oz.	vermouth	30 mL
1 oz.	anisette or anis	30 mL
1 tsp.	white crème de menthe	5 mL

Combine with ice; shake. Strain and add ice.

MAI-TAI I

3 oz.	white rum	90 mL
2 tsp.	lime juice	10 mL
1 tsp.	Triple Sec	5 mL
1 tsp.	almond extract	5 mL
1 tsp.	sugar syrup	5 mL
1	mint sprig	1
1	pineapple stick	1
1	slice lime	1

Combine all except the mint, pineapple stick and lime slice
with ice. Shake. Strain and add lots of ice. Top with mint,
pineapple stick and a lime slice.

MAI-TAI II

2 oz.	Jamaican rum	60 mL
1½ tbsp.	lime juice	20 mL
2 tsp.	Curaçao	10 mL
2 tsp.	apricot brandy	10 mL
1	pineapple stick	1

Combine all, except the pineapple stick, with ice. Shake well; strain and add ice. Top with pineapple stick.

MANHATTAN (DRY)

3 oz.	whiskey	90 mL
1 oz.	dry vermouth	30 mL
1 dash	bitters	1 dash

Stir well with ice, pour in glass, add twist of lemon or cherry.

MANHATTAN

| 1 jigger | bourbon or whiskey | 45 mL |
| ½ oz. | sweet vermouth | 15 mL |

Dash of Angostura bitters, optional. Stir with cracked ice and strain into glass or serve on the rocks.

MARGUARITA

1 jigger	tequila	45 mL
½ oz.	Triple Sec	15 mL
1 oz.	fresh lime or lemon juice	30 mL
	coarse salt	

Moisten cocktail glass rim with fruit rind. Spin rim in the salt. Shake ingredients with cracked ice and strain into glass. Sip over salted rim.

See photograph on cover.

MARTINI (DRY)

3 oz.	gin	90 mL
1 oz.	dry vermouth	30 mL
1 dash	bitters (optional)	1 dash

Stir with ice. Strain. Serve with olive or lemon twist in chilled glass. Combine and serve on ice for Martini On The Rocks. See photograph on cover.

MAUI COCKTAIL

1 oz.	vodka	30 mL
½ oz.	banana liqueur	15 mL
2 tsp.	pineapple juice concentrate	10 mL
1 tsp.	lemon juice	5 mL

Combine with ice; shake well. Strain over crushed ice.

MAXIM'S CHAMPAGNE COCKTAIL

brandied peach, orange
or pineapple
chilled champagne

Place a piece of brandied fruit in champagne glass. Fill glass with champagne.

MILLIONAIRE

| 1 oz. each | rum, apricot brandy, and sloe gin | 30 mL |
| 1 dash | grenadine juice of 1 lime | 1 dash |

Combine with ice; shake. Strain, add ice and serve.

32

MIDORI SPRITZER

1 oz.	Midori melon liqueur	30 mL
2 oz.	dry white wine	60 mL
3 oz.	club soda	90 mL

Pour all ingredients into tall glass over ice. Stir and serve.

MISSISSIPPI MUD

2 large	scoops vanilla ice cream	125 mL
1 jigger	Southern Comfort	45 mL
1 jigger	coffee liqueur	45 mL

Blend ice cream, Southern Comfort and coffee liqueur just until thick. Spoon into cocktail or parfait glass and garnish with shaved chocolate.

MIXED MOCHA FRAPPÉ

¾ oz.	Kahlúa	20 mL
1 tsp.	white crème de menthe	5 mL
1 tsp.	white crème de cacao	5 mL
1 tsp.	Triple Sec	5 mL

Combine without ice and stir. Sugarfrost the rim of glass with water. Pour over crushed ice.

MOSCOW MULE

	juice of ½ lime	
1½ oz.	vodka	45 mL
	ginger ale or ginger beer	
	lime wedge	

Over ice cubes in a mug squeeze lime and add vodka. Top with ginger ale or ginger beer, and garnish with lime wedge.

NECTARINE COOLER

2 oz.	vodka	60 mL
3 oz.	orange juice	90 mL
2 oz.	sliced ripe nectarines	60 mL
1 tsp.	sugar	5 mL
3 oz.	crushed ice	90 mL
	club soda	
1	lemon slice	1

Combine everything except soda and a slice of nectarine, in a blender at low speed for 20 seconds. Strain; add ice and a spritz of soda. Top with the nectarine and a slice of lemon.

OLD FASHIONED

1	lump sugar	1
2 dashes	Angostura bitters	2 dashes
1½ oz.	whisky	45 mL
	soda water	
	orange slice, lemon twist or cherry	

Combine over ice in old fashioned glass. Top with soda water and garnish.
See photograph on cover.

ORANGE BLOSSOM

3 oz.	dry gin	90 mL
1 oz.	orange juice	30 mL
¼ tsp.	powdered sugar or sugar syrup	1 mL
1	orange slice	1

Combine with ice; shake. Strain and add ice. Top with orange slice.

PINA COLADA

2 oz.	gold rum	60 mL
2 oz.	cream of coconut	60 mL
4 oz.	pineapple juice	125 mL
1	pineapple stick	1
1	cherry	1

Combine all but pineapple stick and cherry with ice. Shake well. Strain. Garnish with pineapple and cherry. Can also be mixed with some crushed ice in a blender.
See photograph on cover.

PINEAPPLE DAIQUIRI

1 oz.	white rum	30 mL
2 oz.	pineaple juice	60 mL
1 tsp.	Cointreau	5 mL
½ tsp.	lime juice	2 mL
4 oz.	crushed ice	125 mL

Combine in blender at high speed for 15 seconds. Strain.

PERNOD FLIP

1 oz.	Pernod	30 mL
2 tsp.	Cointreau	10 mL
2 tsp.	lemon juice	10 mL
1½ tsp.	sugar syrup	7 mL
1	egg	1

Combine with ice; shake well. Strain; add ice and serve.

PINK LADY

1 jigger	gin	45 mL
1 oz.	cream or egg white	30 mL
dash	grenadine	dash
1 oz.	lemon juice	30 mL
1 oz.	sugar syrup	30 mL

Combine with ice. Shake very well. Strain and add ice.
See photograph on cover.

PLANTER'S PUNCH

1½ jiggers	Jamaican rum	70 mL
1 oz.	lemon or lime juice	30 mL
1 tsp.	sugar or 1 oz. (30 mL) sugar syrup	5 mL
1 oz.	orange juice several drops grenadine	30 mL

Combine with ice in collins glass. Shake well. Strain onto crushed ice. Garnish with a cherry, lemon or orange slice.

POOP-DECK

1 oz.	brandy	30 mL
½ oz.	port	15 mL
½ oz.	blackberry liqueur	15 mL

Combine with ice; shake well. Strain and add ice.

PRESIDENTE

1½ oz.	white rum	45 mL
1 tbsp.	dry vermouth	15 mL
1-2 dashes	grenadine	1-2 dashes
1-2 dashes	orange Curaçao	1-2 dashes

Combine with ice; shake well. Strain, add ice and serve.

PRINCESS MARY'S PRIDE

½ oz.	French vermouth	15 mL
½ oz.	Dubonnet	15 mL
1 oz.	Calvados	30 mL

Combine with ice; shake well. Strain, add ice and serve.

RASPBERRY FRENCH SPARKLER

½ cup	black raspberry liqueur	125 mL
¼ cup	canned coconut cream	50 mL
2 oz.	vodka	60 mL
16 oz.	vanilla or coconut ice cream	500 mL
1½ cups	chilled sparkling water	375 mL

Combine liqueur, coconut cream and vodka in a blender. Pour equally into 4, 10-12 oz. (300-375 mL) glasses. Scoop ice cream into glasses and pour sparkling water over it. Stir gently and serve immediately with straws and spoons.

RASPBERRY ROYALE FLOAT

10 oz.	pkg. frozen raspberries in syrup, thawed	300 mL
⅔ cup	black raspberry liqueur	150 mL
2½ tbsp.	lemon juice	40 mL
26 oz.	bottle chilled brut champagne	750 mL

Press raspberries and syrup through strainer, discard seeds. Combine raspberry purée, ⅓ cup (75 mL) of liqueur and lemon juice, blend thoroughly. Freeze until firm about 1" (2.5 cm) around the edge and beat to blend thoroughly. Freeze until firm for at least 4 hours. To serve, scoop raspberry mixture equally into 6, 10-12 oz. (300-375 mL) stemmed glasses. Pour a scant tbsp. (15 mL) of the remaining liqueur into each, fill with champagne. Garnish with mint. Serve with spoons.

REGATTA

1 oz.	vodka	30 mL
4 oz.	champagne	125 mL
1-2 dashes	pear brandy	1-2 dashes

Stir together and serve over ice in chilled stemmed glass.

ROB ROY

1 jigger	Scotch	45 mL
⅔ jigger	sweet vermouth	30 mL
2 dashes	Angostura bitters	2 dashes

Combine with ice; shake well. Strain and add ice. Serve with lemon twist.

ROOT BEER

1 oz.	Kahlúa	30 mL
1 oz.	Galliano	30 mL
½ oz.	Kahlúa	15 mL

Pour the 1 oz. (30 mL) Kahlúa and Galliano over ice in tall glass. Fill glass with 7-Up and soda water. Float ½ oz. (15 mL) Kahlúa on top.
See photograph on cover.

RUSSIAN COCKTAIL

¾ oz.	gin	20 mL
¾ oz.	vodka	20 mL
1 tbsp.	white créme de cacao	15 mL

Combine with ice; shake well. Strain, add ice and serve.

RUSTY NAIL

1 oz.	Scotch	30 mL
1 oz.	Drambuie	30 mL
	lemon peel	

Serve on the rocks in old fashioned glass.
See photograph on cover.

SCARLET O'HARA I

2 oz.	Southern Comfort	60 mL
1 oz.	lemon juice	30 mL
1 dash	grenadine	1 dash
	soda water	

Combine with ice; shake well. Strain, add ice, fill with soda. See photograph page 16.

SCARLET O'HARA II

1½ oz.	Southern Comfort	45 mL
½	peach, soaked in brandy	½
3 tsp.	lime juice	15 mL
3	maraschino cherries	3
3 oz.	crushed ice	90 mL

Combine in blender at a high speed for 15 seconds. Strain. Serve in highball glass.

SCOFF-LAW COCKTAIL

1 dash	orange bitters	1 dash
1 oz.	Canadian whiskey	30 mL
1 oz.	dry vermouth	30 mL
⅓ oz.	lemon juice	10 mL
⅓ oz.	grenadine	10 mL

Shake well with ice. Strain, add ice and serve.

SCORPION

2 oz.	white rum	60 mL
2 oz.	orange juice	60 mL
1 oz.	brandy	30 mL
2 tbsp.	lemon juice	30 mL
2 tsp.	almond extract	10 mL
3 oz.	crushed ice	90 mL

Combine in blender at a low speed for 15 seconds. Strain and add ice. Garnish with orange slice. Serve in collins glass.

SCREWDRIVER

Place in highball glass

2	ice cubes	2
1½ oz.	vodka	45 mL

Fill with fresh orange juice and garnish with cherries and fruit.

See photograph on cover.

SEA FOAM

4-5	ice cubes	4-5
	juice of 1 lime or lemon	
½ tsp.	sugar or sugar syrup	2 mL
1	egg white	1
2 oz.	vodka	60 mL

Put 4-5 ice cubes into cocktail shaker. Pour the juice, sugar or sugar syrup, egg white and vodka over ice. Shake until a frost forms. Strain and pour into a sour glass. To make a pink Sea Foam substitute 1 tsp. (5 mL) grenadine syrup for the ½ tsp. (2 mL) sugar.

SHAMROCK

1 oz.	Irish whiskey	30 mL
1 oz.	dry vermouth	30 mL
3 dashes	each green Chartreuse	3 dashes
	and crème de menthe	
1	green olive	1

Stir with ice. Strain, add ice and serve with green olive.

SIDECAR

1½ oz.	brandy	45 mL
¾ oz.	Cointreau	20 mL
¾ oz.	lemon juice	20 mL

Shake well with ice. Strain, add ice and serve.

SILVER DOLLAR

1 oz.	crème de banana	30 mL
1 oz.	white crème de menthe	30 mL
1 oz.	light cream	30 mL

Shake well with ice. Strain. Serve in old fashioned glass with ice.

SILVER STALLION

1 oz.	dry gin	30 mL
1 oz.	vanilla ice cream	30 mL
	juice of ½ lemon and	
	½ lime	

Shake with a little fine ice. Strain. Add ice and fill with soda.

SINGAPORE SLING

1½ oz.	gin	45 mL
1 tsp.	sherry brandy	5 mL
1 tsp.	grenadine	5 mL
1½ oz.	lemon	45 mL
1 dash	Angostura bitters	1 dash
	soda water or ginger	
	beer	

Shake with ice cubes. Strain, and add ice, mint, orange and cherry garnish. Top with soda water or ginger beer.
See photograph page 16.

SPRITZER

| 5 oz. | white or red wine | 150 mL |
| | club soda | |

Thoroughly chill wine and soda. Pour wine into a large goblet; add ice and fill with soda. Stir. Garnish with lemon peel.
See photograph on cover.

STINGER

| 2 oz. | brandy | 60 mL |
| 1 oz. | white crème de menthe | 30 mL |

Shake well with ice; strain into an old fashioned glass with cracked ice.

SUFFERING BAR STEWARD

2 oz.	cognac	60 mL
2 oz.	dry sherry	60 mL
	ginger ale	

In a tall tumbler put cognac and dry sherry. Fill with ginger ale. Garnish with sprig fresh mint.

SUN SPLASH

1 splash	vodka	1 splash
3 oz.	red wine	90 mL
2 dashes	orange Curaçao	2 dashes

Stir over ice, strain.

SURF RIDER

4-5	ice cubes	4-5
	juice of ½ lemon	
	juice of 1 orange	
	OR	
4 tbsp.	canned unsweetened juice	60 mL
½ tsp.	grenadine	2 mL
1 oz.	sweet vermouth	30 mL
2 oz.	vodka	60 mL

Put 4-5 ice cubes into a cocktail shaker. Pour the lemon juice, orange juice, grenadine, sweet vermouth and vodka over ice. Shake until frost forms. Strain and pour in sour glass.

TEQUILA RICKEY

1½ oz.	tequila	45 mL
1 tsp.	lime juice	5 mL
	club soda	
	lime and orange slices	
	salt	

Pour the tequila and lime juice into a highball glass; add ice and stir well. Fill the glass with soda. Twist in the slice of lime. Sprinkle a bit of salt over the drink. Garnish with orange slice.

TEQUILA SUNRISE

1½ oz.	tequila	45 mL
¾ oz.	grenadine	20 mL
	orange juice	

Combine first 2 ingredients. Fill glass with juice. Garnish with orange slice and cherry.

TOM COLLINS

1½ oz.	gin	45 mL
1 tsp.	sugar syrup	5 mL
2 tsp.	lemon juice	10 mL
	soda to fill	

Combine everything except soda; stir well and add ice. Fill the glass with soda and garnish with orange slice and cherry. See photograph page 16.

VELVET HAMMER

½ oz.	brandy	15 mL
1 oz.	crème de cacao	30 mL
4 oz.	cream	125 mL

Combine with ice; shake very well. Strain. Serve in cocktail glass.

VERMOUTH

| 2 cups | dry white wine | 500 mL |
| 1 tsp. | wormwood extract | 5 mL |

Combine in a bottle. Seal, shake, and allow to stand until the wormwood ferments in the wine.

VODKA SLING

2 oz.	vodka	60 mL
1½ tsp.	Benedictine	45 mL
1½ tsp.	cherry brandy	7 mL
1 tsp.	lemon juice	5 mL
few dashes	each Angostura and orange bitters	few dashes
	club soda	

Combine everything, except the soda, with ice. Shake well. Strain; add ice and fill the glass with soda.

WHISKEY SOUR

3 oz.	whiskey	90 mL
	juice of ½ lemon	
½ tsp.	sugar	2 mL
	shake with ice	

Serve in Delmonico glass. Add cherry and orange slice. See photograph on cover.

WHITE LION

1½ oz.	rum	45 mL
	juice of ½ lemon	
1 tsp.	powdered sugar	5 mL
12-15 drops	each Angostura bitters and raspberry syrup	12-15 drops

Shake with ice and serve.

44

WIDOW'S DREAM

3 oz.	Benedictine	90 mL
1	egg	1
1½ oz.	cream	45 mL

Shake well with ice, strain, add ice and serve with 2 short straws.

WINNER'S DREAM

1 oz.	dark rum	30 mL
1 oz.	Cointreau	30 mL
1½ tsp.	lemon	7 mL

Shake well with ice, strain and serve over crushed ice.

ZOMBIE

1½ oz.	gold rum	45 mL
1 tbsp.	lime juice	15 mL
1 tbsp.	Jamaican rum	15 mL
1 tbsp.	white rum	15 mL
1 tbsp.	each pineapple and papaya juice	15 mL
1½ tsp.	sugar syrup	7 mL
1 tsp.	151-proof rum	5 mL
1	pineapple stick granulated sugar	1

Combine everything except the high-proof rum, pineapple stick and sugar with ice. Shake well. Strain and add ice. Garnish with the pineapple stick and a cherry. Float the high-proof rum and sprinkle a little sugar over it.

SAKE

To a 5-gallon (20 L) crock add the following ingredients:

4 lb.	Delta rice	2 kg
2 lb.	dark Sunmaid raisins	1 kg
1 lb.	light raisins	500 g
12 lb.	sugar	6 kg
2	pkg. yeast	2

Cover ingredients in crock to within ½ (1.2 cm) of top with lukewarm water. Cut hole about 2″ (5 cm) in diameter in a piece of well-burnt toast. Place this on top of another piece of well-burnt toast. Float this raft on top of the solution and put 2 packages of yeast in the cavity of the raft. Have crock placed in a location which has a very steady warmth.

Stir twice daily for 4 days. Then leave undisturbed for 10 days. (It is beneficial to squeeze raisins by hand after they have become swollen, say second or third day) Keep liquid topped to the ½″ (1.2 cm) mark from top of container. At end of fourth day carefully remove toast and yeast. On fourteenth day skim off raisins and siphon sake into gallon jugs, using a strainer on crock end of hose to prevent any possibility of bits of raisin or rice entering jars. Just over 4 gallons of sake should be obtained. Leave screw caps of jars loose for 1 week. Store in cool place. This helps sake to stop working and clear.

Sake is ready to drink from the day it is run from crock but improves as it clears. When jars are clear and sediment has settled, siphon into smaller bottles, being careful not to disturb the sediment.

BEER

10 gallons	water	40 L
2 oz.	Fugal Hops	55 g
2½-3 cans	Gold Medal Plain Malt	3.75 kg
5 lbs.	sugar	2.5 kg
2 tsp.	table salt	10 mL
2 tsp.	Gypsum	10 mL
2 tsp.	copper finings	10 mL
1	pkg. Bottom Ferment Yeast	1

Boil as much water as possible. Use hops that are green and in bulk form (loose). Place hops in cheesecloth or something similar. Add next 6 ingredients, stirring frequently to stop additives from burning on bottom. Boil for 1½ hours. Skim off brown sludge on top of brew; this is protein from malt.

After brew has boiled for awhile take some of the boiling mixture and fill a 1 gallon (4 L) plastic jug a little less than ½ full; add 5 tsp. (25 mL) sugar. Cool to below 70 F, then add yeast. Stir well, put burper in top of jug and store in cool area, such as a refrigerator.

After mixture has boiled add water to make 10 gallons (40 L). Cool brew to below 70°F (21°C) add yeast starter and stir well. Check with hydrometer, which should read 1040. Cover and let it die off to approximately 1020. This takes about 3 days. Siphon into another container and let this die down to 1005-1004, then bottle, adding 1 tsp. (5 mL) of sugar per bottle. Cap and store 4-5 weeks. Cool and enjoy.

Makes approximately 10 cases of beer.

See photograph page 80.

LAGER BEER

2		campden pills	2
		beer fermenter (plastic garbage can)	
5	gallons	water	20 L
2	tbsp.	coarse salt (pickling salt)	25 mL
5	lbs.	white sugar	2.5 kg
2½	lb.	can Gold Medal Malt, plain-light	1.25 kg
1¾	oz.	compressed hops (4-oz. (113 g) pkg. green)	50 mL
2	tbsp.	citric acid or lemon juice	25 mL
5	tsp.	yeast nutrient (wine art)	25 mL
1		pkg. Lager Beer Yeast balling hydrometer	

Dissolve 2 campden pills in water as pkg. instructions. Rinse out beer fermenter and save the campden water for rinsing bottles and caps later. Boil water in 2 containers, adding salt to 1. After water has boiled pour 1 container of water over the sugar and malt which has been placed in beer fermenter. Place hops in cheesecloth and tie up. Place hops in the other container and continue boiling for 30 minutes. Remove hops from water and pour into beer fermenter; stir well and cool down to 72°F (21°C). Add citric acid and nutrient; stir and add yeast. Hydrometer reading should be 1040. If hydrometer reading is below 1040 add sugar, if above 1040 add water. Cover fermenter with plastic sheet well tied down. Next day remove scum from top. After 3-4 days test with hydrometer daily until reading falls to 1020. Siphon off into secondary container or fermenter. Keep covered with plastic and check daily for hydrometer reading. When beer has reached 1004, bottle, add 1 tsp. (5 mL) sugar to each bottle. Cap and store in cool dark place for at least 2 weeks.

Bottles should be well washed and sterilized.

Yields approximately 5 cases of beer.

ALMOND LIQUEUR

1½	lemons, yellow peel only	1½
½"	piece cinnamon stick	1.2 cm
4	whole cloves	4
¼ tsp.	caraway seeds	1 mL
2½ cups	vodka	625 mL
1¼ cups	sugar	300 mL
1¼ cups	water	300 mL
2 cups	almond milk	500 mL

Slice lemon peel, and place in a tightly sealed jar with cinnamon, cloves, caraway and vodka for 5 days. Dissolve the sugar in boiling water; cool, and add it to the contents of jar. Mix thoroughly; let stand for 2 more days, then add the almond milk. (See below). Mix thoroughly and let stand for 15 more days in a cool dark place, filter through cheesecloth and return to cool, dark place for 1½ months. Filter once more to remove the sediment.

Almond Milk can be prepared by grinding or shredding 6 oz. (170 g) of blanched almonds in a blender. Combine with 6 oz. (170 g) of sugar, and 12 oz. (375 mL) distilled water. Shake mixture until sugar is dissolved.

AMARETTO LIQUEUR I

3 cups	vodka	750 mL
½ tsp.	ground cinnamon	2 mL
½ tsp.	ground coriander	2 mL
2 cups	crushed peach pits,	500 mL
2 cups	sugar	500 mL
1 cup	water	250 mL

Steep the vodka, spices and crushed pits for 2 months then strain. Boil the sugar and water until dissolved. Cool and add to peach pit mixture. Leave until clear. Bottle and store.

AMARETTO LIQUEUR II

2 tbsp.	Amaretto extract	25 mL
1½ cups	sugar	375 mL
6 tsp.	Smoothy Crystals	30 mL
	vodka	

Combine extract, sugar and crystals in blender or electric beater. Add vodka to the 32 oz. (1 L) mark on blender (4 cups). Blend at low speed until sugar and crystals are dissolved. Bottle. Improves with age.

ANISETTE LIQUEUR

5 tbsp.	crushed anise seed	75 mL
1½ tsp.	crushed fennel seed	7 mL
1½ tsp.	ground coriander	7 mL
1 cup	honey	250 mL
3 cups	brandy	750 mL

Combine the brandy and spices and steep for 3 weeks, shaking the jar occasionally. Strain through a cloth several times and stir in the honey. Let stand until clear. Bottle and store.

APRICOT BRANDY I

2 tbsp.	Apricot Extract	25 mL
1½ cups	sugar	375 mL
6 tsp.	Smoothy Crystals	30 mL
	vodka	

Combine extract, sugar and crystals in blender, or electric beater. Add vodka to the 32 oz. (1 L) mark on blender (4 cups.). Blend at low speed until sugar and crystals are dissolved. Bottle. Improves with age.

APRICOT BRANDY II

1 lb.	apricots	500 g
1 lb.	sugar	500 g
4 oz.	brandy	125 mL

Boil the apricots whole in enough water to cover them. Lower heat and simmer until tender. Remove the skins. Boil the sugar in enough water to make a syrup and pour it over the apricots. Allow to stand for at least 1 day. Pour mixture into a jug or large bottle and add the brandy. Seal, and store a year. Strain and bottle.

APRICOT LIQUEUR

⅔ cup	thick apricot jam	150 mL
3½ cups	brandy	875 mL
2 tbsp.	honey	30 mL

In a blender whip the jam and brandy. Put in a tightly sealed jar and store in a warm spot for 6 weeks. Strain through cheese-cloth and add honey, mixing well. Leave until clear.

BAILEY'S IRISH CREAM

10 oz. can	sweetened condensed milk	300 mL
2 cups	table cream	500 mL
2	eggs	2
2 tbsp.	chocolate syrup	30 mL
1 tsp.	almond extract	5 mL
8 oz.	whiskey	250 mL

Combine in blender on low until well mixed.
Store in refrigerator. Will keep for 1 week.
See photograph page 48.

BENEDICTINE

2 tbsp.	Reverendine Extract	25 mL
1¼ cup	sugar	300 mL
6 tsp.	Smoothy Crystals	30 mL
	brandy	

Combine extract, sugar and crystals in blender or electric beater. Add brandy to the 32-oz. (1 mL) mark on blender. Blend at low speed until sugar and crystals are dissolved. Bottle. Improves with age.

BLACKCURRANT BRANDY

| ¾ cup | blackcurrants | 175 mL |
| 3 cups | brandy | 750 mL |

Place the blackcurrants and brandy in a glass jar. Seal tightly and store in a cool, dark place for 8 months. Strain and bottle.

BRANDY ALEXANDER LIQUEUR

10 oz.	can sweetened condensed milk	300 mL
1 cup	table cream	250 mL
1 cup	brandy	250 mL
½ cup	crème de cacao	125 mL
2	eggs	2
	nutmeg	

Mix all ingredients together in a blender until smooth. Keep refrigerated and shake before pouring. Will keep up to 1 week. Sprinkle nutmeg on top of drink before serving.

Makes about 4 cups (1 L).

CANDY CANE

10 oz.	Kahlúa	300 mL
8 oz.	peppermint schnapps	250 mL
6 oz.	Irish cream	175 mL
4 cups	milk	1 L

Place a dozen ice cubes in a medium bowl and pour in the Kahlúa, schnapps, Irish cream and milk. Stir and serve in punch glasses. Sprinkle with nutmeg.

CHERRY BRANDY I

3 cups	cherries	750 mL
3 cups	brandy	750 mL
½ cup	sugar	125 mL

Pierce cherries with a fork, and with 2 cups (500 mL) brandy put in glass jar. Leave for 1 month, then strain. Add remaining brandy and sugar. Stir well to dissolve the sugar, and let sit until clear.

CHERRY BRANDY II

2 tbsp.	Cherry Brandy Extract	25 mL
1 cup	sugar	250 mL
5 tsp.	Smoothy Crystals	30 mL
	brandy	

Combine extract, sugar and crystals in blender or electric beater. Add brandy to the 32-oz. (L) mark on blender. Blend at low speed until sugar and crystals are dissolved. Bottle. Improves with age.

CHOCOLATE MINT LIQUEUR

10 oz.	sweetened condensed milk	300 mL
1 cup	milk	250 mL
½ cup	crème de cacao	125 mL
½ cup	crème de menthe	125 mL
½ cup	alcohol	125 mL
¼ cup	chocolate syrup	50 mL
1 tsp.	vanilla	5 mL
2 tsp.	peppermint flavoring	10 mL

Mix all ingredients together in a blender until smooth. Keep refrigerated and shake before pouring. Store refrigerated for up to one week.

COCONUT LIQUEUR

2 cups	fresh coconut meat	500 mL
4	coriander leaves	4
4	juniper berries	4
2½ cups	brandy	625 mL
1 cup	vodka	250 mL

Cut the coconut into small pieces and add to rest of ingredients in a glass jar. Seal tightly and leave for 3 weeks in a cool dark place. Gently shake from time to time. Then strain through a paper filter into a glass jar and seal tightly. Return to the cool, dark place and leave for 3 months.

COGNAC

¾ cup	sugar	175 mL
6 tsp.	Smoothy Crystals	30 mL
2 tbsp.	bottle Eau De Vie Jaune Extract	25 mL
	vodka	

Combine extract, sugar and crystals in blender or electric beater. Add vodka to the 4-cup (1 L) mark on blender. Blend at low speed until sugar and crystals are dissolved. Bottle. Improves with age.

See photograph page 48.

COINTREAU

2 tbsp.	Triple Sec or Curaçao Extract	25 mL
1 cup	sugar	250 mL
6 tsp.	Smoothy Crystals Vodka	30 mL

Combine extract, sugar and crystals in blender or electric beater. Add vodka to the 4-cup (1 L) mark. Blend at low speed until sugar and crystals are dissolved. Bottle. Improves with age.

CRÈME DE CACAO I

1 lb.	cacao beans	500 g
2 x 26 oz.	brandy	2 x 750 mL
2 cups	sugar	500 mL
1 tbsp.	vanilla extract	15 mL

Roast the beans until nearly charred; soak in the brandy for 1 week. Boil the sugar in water to make a thick syrup; allow it to cool, then combine with the brandy. Add the vanilla extract; strain and bottle.

CRÈME DE CACAO II

2 tbsp.	Cacao extract	25 mL
1¼ cup	sugar	300 mL
6 tsp.	Smoothy Crystals Vodka	30 mL

Combine extract, sugar and crystal in blender or electric beater. Add vodka to the 4-cup (1 L) mark on blender. Blend at low speed until sugar and crystals are dissolved. Bottle. Improves with age.

CRÉME DE MENTHE I

1½ cups	crushed fresh mint leaves	375 mL
3 cups	vodka	750 mL
1 cup	sugar	250 mL
½ cup	water	125 mL
4 tbsp.	Glucose Solids	60 mL

Put leaves in a large jar and cover with vodka. Steep for 48 hours and strain. Boil sugar, water and Glucose Solids until dissolved. When cool, add to mint liqueur and leave until clear. Bottle.

CRÈME DE MENTHE II

2 tbsp.	Menthe Verte Extract	25 mL
1¼ cups	sugar	300 mL
6 tsp.	Smoothy Crystals	30 mL
	vodka	

Combine extract, sugar and crystals in blender. Add vodka to 4-cup (1 L) mark on blender. Blend on low until crystals dissolved. Bottle.

See photograph page 48.

CURAÇAO

4	oranges	4
1 cup	liquid honey	250 mL
3 cups	bourbon	750 mL

Remove the outer peel from the oranges without any of the white pith. Steep the peel in the bourbon for 1 month, strain and add honey. Let stand until clear and bottle.

DRAMBUIE

½ cup	sugar	125 mL
6 tsp.	Smoothy Crystals	30 mL
½ cup	water	125 mL
2 tbsp.	Lorbuis Extract	25 mL
3½ cups	Scotch	875 mL

Combine all ingredients in blender on low. Blend well and bottle. Improves with age.

FRUIT LIQUEUR

2 cups	strawberries	500 mL
2 cups	raspberries	500 mL
2 cups	gooseberries	500 mL
2 cups	huckleberries or elderberries	500 mL
1½ cups	sugar	375 mL
3 cups	vodka	750 mL

Crush the fruit in a bowl, mix well with the sugar and place in the refrigerator for 5 hours. Transfer the pulp and juices to a jar and add the vodka. Seal tightly and store for 3 weeks. Strain through cheesecloth until clear, into a glass jar. Seal tightly and store in a cool dark place for 6 months.

GALLIANO

1 cup	sugar	250 mL
½ cup	water	125 mL
8 tsp.	Smoothy Crystals	40 mL
2 tbsp.	Genepy Jaune Extract	25 mL
3 cups	vodka	750 mL

Boil sugar, water and crystals until dissolved. Cool and add extract and vodka.
See photograph page 48 and on cover.

GRAND MARNIER

1 cup	sugar	250 mL
2 tbsp.	Orange Brandy Extract	25 mL
6 tsp.	Smoothy Crystals	30 mL
	brandy	

Combine extract, sugar and crystals in blender or electric beater. Add brandy to the 4-cup (1 L) mark on blender. Blend on low speed until sugar and crystals are dissolved. Bottle. Improves with age.

See photograph page 48.

IRISH CREAM

2 tbsp.	Irish Cream Extract	25 mL
1½ cups	sugar	375 mL
6 tsp.	Smoothy Crystals	30 mL
	Irish whiskey	

Combine extract, sugar and crystals in blender or electric beater. Add whiskey to the 4-cup (1 L) mark. Blend at low speed until sugar and crystals are dissolved. Bottle. Improves with age. Serve half and half with cream.

KAHLÚA I

2 tbsp.	Moka Extract	25 mL
1½ oz.	sugar	375 mL
6 tsp.	Smoothy Crystals	30 mL
	vodka	

Combine extract, sugar and crystals in blender or electric beater. Add vodka to the 4-cup (1 L) mark on blender. Blend at low speed until sugar and crystals are dissolved. Bottle. Improves with age.

See photograph page 48.

KAHLÚA II

3¼ cups	white sugar	800 mL
1½ cups	hot water	375 mL
½ cup	boiling water	125 mL
2 oz.	instant coffee	60 mL
26 oz.	vodka	750 mL
	vanilla bean, halved lengthwise	

Boil sugar and 1½ cups (375 mL) water for 7-10 minutes. Combine ½ cup (125 mL) boiling water and instant coffee. Add to syrup mixture. Cool, add vodka and put in 2, 26 oz. (750 mL) bottles; put ½ vanilla bean in each bottle. Cap and leave 2 weeks. Remove vanilla bean.

Vanilla bean may be rinsed off, dried and used again.

KIRSCH I

4½ cups	unpitted sour cherries	1 L
1 cup	sugar	250 mL
4 cups	vodka	1 L

Cut up the cherries and remove the pits. Wrap the pits in a cloth and smash with a hammer. Put the cherries, pits and vodka in a tightly sealed jar. Let steep for 4 weeks, and then strain. Add the sugar and shake until it is dissolved. Let stand for 1 week.

KIRSCH II

2 tbsp.	Kirsch extract	25 mL
4 tsp.	Smoothy Crystals	20 mL
	vodka	

Combine extract and crystals in blender or electric beater. Add vodka to the 4-cup (1 L) mark. Blend at low speed until crystals are dissolved. Bottle. Improves with age.

KUMMEL

2 tbsp.	caraway seeds	30 mL
3 tsp.	fennel seeds	15 mL
1½ tsp.	cumin	7 mL
26 oz.	vodka	750 mL
1 cup	sugar syrup	250 mL

Crush the caraway and fennel seeds; add to the cumin and vodka. Steep for 1½ weeks, then strain out the seeds. Add sugar syrup.

LEMON AND ORANGE LIQUEUR

4	oranges, orange part of peel only	4
4	lemons, yellow part of peel only	4
¾ cup	sugar	200 mL
4 cups	brandy	1 L
1 cup	sweet sparkling wine	250 mL
1 cup	vodka	250 mL

Slice the lemon and orange peel and add to all other ingredients in a glass jar. Let sit for 3 months, then strain through a paper filter into a glass jar and seal tightly. Store in a cool, dark place for 6 months.

MOGUL BASHER

8 oz.	Kahlúa	250 mL
6 oz.	Irish cream	175 mL
6 oz.	banana liqueur	175 mL

Mix all ingredients and pour equal amounts into 6 sugar-rimmed brandy snifters. Top with whipped cream and chocolate shavings.

MAGIC CANADIAN CREAM

10 oz.	can sweetened condensed milk	300 mL
13 oz.	can evaporated milk	385 mL
1½ tsp.	chocolate syrup	7 mL
1 tbsp.	instant coffee granules	15 mL
2	eggs	2
1 cup	brandy or rye whisky	250 mL

Combine all ingredients in blender, blend until smooth. Transfer to glass bottle, seal and refrigerate.
Makes 4 cups (1 L).

MAGIC GROG

10 oz.	can sweetened condensed milk	300 mL
2½ cups	water	625 mL
1 cup	brandy	250 mL
½ cup	dark rum	125 mL
2	egg whites	2
	nutmeg	

In a small punch bowl or pitcher combine milk and water. Stir in brandy and rum. Set aside. Beat egg whites to very soft peaks. Stir into milk mixture. Chill. Garnish with nutmeg.
Makes 6 cups (1.5 L).

ORANGE OR LEMON BRANDY

3 cups	brandy	750 mL
1 cup	sugar	250 mL
1 large	orange or lemon	1

Pour brandy into large jar or container with tight-fitting lid. Add sugar. Stir until dissolved. Wash orange or lemon and dry thoroughly. With vegetable parer remove peel in 1 long continuous spiral. Add to brandy mixture in tightly covered jar and set aside, away from light for 1 week to allow flavor to develop. Strain, and bottle. Improves with age.
Makes 3½ cups (875 mL).

ORANGE BRANDY

6 large	oranges	6
3 oz.	orange blossoms	85 g
14 cups	brandy	3.5 L
8 cups	sugar	2 L

Peel the oranges and squeeze out the juice; combine the peels, juice and orange blossoms with the brandy in a jar; seal and allow to stand for at least 1 week. Boil the sugar in enough water to make a syrup; add to the brandy when ready. Strain and bottle for future use.

PEACH BRANDY

10 large	peaches	10
1 cup	sugar	250 mL
2 cups	brandy	500 mL

Slice the fruit; remove the pit; crush the kernels from the center of the pit and combine with the sliced fruit, brandy and sugar in a large jar or bottles. Store at room temperature for a month, shaking daily. After 1 month strain, bottle, and store for another 6 months before using.

RASPBERRY BRANDY

2 tbsp.	Framboise Extract	25 mL
1¼ cups	sugar	300 mL
6 tsp.	Smoothy Crystals	30 mL
	vodka	

Combine extract, sugar and crystals in blender or electric beater. Add vodka to the 4-cup (1 L) mark. Blend at low speed until sugar and crystals are dissolved. Bottle. Improves with age.

See photograph page 48.

RASPBERRY LIQUEUR

3 cups	raspberries	750 mL
15	cherry leaves	15
2½ cups	sugar	625 mL
½	lemon, sliced yellow peel only	½
2½ cups	vodka	625 mL

Put all ingredients in a tightly sealed jar and put in the sun for 1 month, shaking occasionally. Then place in cool, dark place for 5 months. Strain through colander then cheesecloth into a glass jar and seal well. Return to cool dark place for 1 more month. Delicious.

RUM CREAM LIQUEUR

10 oz.	can sweetened condensed milk	300 mL
1½ cups	rum	375 mL
1 cup	table cream	250 mL
2	eggs	2
2 tbsp.	chocolate syrup	30 mL
2 tsp.	vanilla	10 mL

Mix all ingredients together in a blender until smooth. Keep refrigerated and shake before pouring. Will keep 1 week.

SWEETENED CONDENSED MILK

¼ cup	hot tap water	50 mL
¾ cup	granulated sugar	175 mL
1¼ cups	dry skim milk powder	300 mL

Mix in blender about 1 minute or until sugar has partially dissolved the water and sugar. While continuing to blend, slowly add dry skim milk powder. Cover and refrigerate. This makes 1½ cups (375 mL) and can be used in any recipe calling for this type of milk, but must be stored in the refrigerator for 24 hours before using to develop the flavor. Do not store longer than 1 week.

TIA MARIA I

2″ piece	vanilla bean	5 cm
2 cups	sugar	500 mL
1½ cups	water	375 mL
¼ cup	dry instant coffee	50 mL
½ cup	boiling water	125 mL
2 cups	dark rum	500 mL

Cut the vanilla bean into 3 pieces. Add to the sugar and 1½ cups water, and boil for 15 minutes. Let cool. Dissolve the coffee in ½ cup of boiling water, mixing with the sugar mixture and the rum. Seal and shake well. Let sit for 2 weeks.

TIA MARIA II

2 tbsp.	café sport extract	25 mL
¾ cup	sugar	175 mL
1 oz.	Smoothy Crystals	30 mL
26 oz.	vodka	750 mL
½ tsp.	vanilla	2 mL

Mix in blender on low until sugar is dissolved. Bottle.

TIA MARIA III

2¼ cups	white sugar	550 mL
2 cups	water	500 mL
1 tbsp.	dry instant coffee	15 mL
26 oz.	vodka	750 mL

Boil sugar and water for 5 minutes. Add instant coffee. Stir in vodka. Pour in bottle and chill.

AFTER EIGHT

8 oz.	crème de menthe	250 mL
6 oz.	Kahlúa	175 mL
6 oz.	Irish cream	175 mL
5 cups	coffee	1.25 L
	whipped cream	
	chocolate shavings	

Combine crème de menthe, Kahlúa and Irish cream. Pour equal amounts into 6 sugar-rimmed brandy snifters. Add 4-6 oz. (125-175 mL) of coffee to each. Top with fresh whipped cream and sprinkle with chocolate shavings.

ALMOND GLOGG

2 cups	water	500 mL
1 tsp.	whole allspice	5 mL
3 x 2" (5 cm)	cinnamon sticks, broken	3
3 bags	almond herbal tea	3
2 tbsp.	brown sugar	30 mL
¾ cup	light rosé wine	175 mL
1 tbsp.	raisins	15 mL
4	blanched almonds	4

In a medium saucepan, bring water, allspice and cinnamon to a boil; simmer 5 minutes. Add tea bags and sugar; steep 5 minutes. Place wine, raisins and almonds in heat-proof container. Pour tea mixture through strainer into container.
Serves 4. (Calories 60)

BLACK IRISH TEA

3 cups	boiling water	750 mL
6	blackcurrant tea bags or ½ cup (175 mL) loose blackcurrant tea	6
1 cup	crème de cassis (blackcurrant liqueur)	250 mL
1 cup	heavy cream, softly whipped	250 mL

BLACK IRISH TEA (cont'd)

1 tbsp.	confectioner's sugar	15 mL
	blackcurrant preserves	

Pour water over tea in kettle and let steep 5 minutes. strain if using loose tea. Stir tea and liqueur in 6 heat-proof glasses. Whip cream with sugar until it holds soft peaks. Spoon cream on top of hot tea. Drizzle with blackcurrant preserves.

See photograph page 64.

CAFÉ BRÛLOT I

43 x 1" (2.5 cm)	lemon peel strips	43
23 x 1" (2.5 cm)	orange peel strips	23
2"	cinnamon stick, broken	5 cm
1 tbsp.	sugar	15 mL
1 tsp.	whole allspice	5 mL
2 tbsp.	bourbon or brandy	25 mL
1 cup	strong hot coffee	250 mL

In center of a large skillet, place first 5 ingredients. Warm brandy in small saucepan; carefully ignite. Pour over ingredients in skillet. When flame dies out, add coffee, stirring to dissolve sugar. Serve in demitasse cups.

Serves 4. (Calories-200)

CAFÉ BRÛLOT II

3 strips	orange peel	3
	super-fine sugar	
3 tbsp.	warmed cognac or brandy	45 mL
	hot strong coffee	
1	cinnamon stick	1

Rub the rim of a heat-proof glass with 1 orange strip; dip rim of glass in sugar. Twist 1 strip orange into glass. Add cognac or brandy with a spoon set in glass to prevent glass from cracking. Ignite cognac or brandy and slowly pour in coffee to fill glass. Add a cinnamon stick and top with whipped cream. Garnish with remaining orange strip.

Makes 1 serving.

CAFÉ BRÛLOT III

½ cup	dry instant coffee	125 mL
4 cups	boiling water	1 L
3	cinnamon sticks	3
1 tbsp.	whole cloves	15 mL
⅓ to ½ cup	sugar	75-125 mL
½ cup	brandy	125 mL
	peel from 1 orange and 1 lemon, slivered	

Dissolve coffee in boiling water. Add cinnamon and cloves. Cover and let stand 15 minutes. Strain and reheat. Meanwhile, combine remaining ingredients in chafing dish. Heat, then slowly add coffee. Ladle into demitasse cups.

Makes 4½ cup (1 L) or 9, 4-oz. (125 mL) servings.

CAFÉ ROYAL

	hot strong coffee	
1	sugar cube	1
1 tbsp.	warmed cognac or brandy	15 mL

Pour coffee into demitasse or coffee cup. Hold a spoon with cognac-soaked sugar cube above cup. Ignite with a match and when flame dies down lower spoon into cup then stir gently.

CAPE COD TODDY

1 cup	cranberry juice cocktail	250 mL
1 cup	water	250 mL
3 2" (5 cm)	cinnamon sticks	3
2 tsp.	brown sugar	10 mL
1	tea bag	1
¼ cup	vodka	50 mL
4	lime wedges	4

In saucepan, combine first 4 ingredients. Bring to a boil, reduce heat and simmer 5 minutes. Add tea bag, steep 3 minutes. Pour through strainer into small, heat-proof pitcher; discard tea bag and cinnamon. Stir in vodka, garnish with lime.

Serves 4.

COFFEE CARIOCA

2	oranges, peeled	2
½ cup	dry instant coffee	125 mL
¼ cup	sugar	50 mL
4 cups	boiling water	1 L
¼ cup	rum	50 mL
	sweetened whipped cream	

Remove all white membrane from oranges. Slice into ¼" slices and remove seeds. Place in large heat-proof bowl with the coffee and sugar. Stir in the boiling water. Let stand 30 minutes. Strain coffee into saucepan, heat almost to boiling. Remove from heat and stir in rum. Serve in demitasse cups topped with sweetened whipped cream. If desired, garnish with grated orange rind and shaved chocolate or cinnamon.

COFFEE NUDGE

8 oz.	brandy	250 mL
6 oz.	coffee liqueur	175 mL
6 oz.	white cacao	175 mL
5 cups	coffee	1.25 L
	whipped cream	
	chocolate shavings	

Mix the brandy with the coffee liqueur and white cacao. Pour equal amounts into 6, sugar-rimmed brandy snifters and add 4-6 oz. (125-175 mL) of coffee. Top with fresh whipped cream and sprinkle with chocolate shavings.

DELTA SUPREME

10 oz.	cognac	300 mL
8 oz.	Cointreau	250 mL
8 oz.	Kahlúa	250 mL
5 cups	coffee	1.25 L
	whipped cream	
	chocolate shavings	

Mix the cognac with the Cointreau and Kahlúa. Pour equal amounts into 6 sugar-rimmed brandy snifters and add 6 oz. (175 mL) of coffee each. Top with fresh whipped cream and sprinkle with chocolate shavings.

ESPRESSO GALLIANO

	hot espresso coffee	
1 tbsp.	Galliano	15 mL
1 strip	lemon peel	1

To each demitasse cup of coffee, add Galliano. Twist lemon peel over cup and drop in.
Makes 1 serving.

FLAMING COFFEE

Dim lights before the flaming starts.

3 cups	hot strong coffee	750 mL
2 tbsp.	sugar	30 mL
1	lemon rind in 1 piece	1
1 cup	gold rum	250 mL
	whipped cream	
	shaved chocolate	

Heat coffee, sugar and lemon rind in saucepan. Add rum and set aflame. When flame dies, ladle into heat-proof cups and top with whipped cream and shaved chocolate. Serve at once.
Makes 6 servings.

HAPPY ENDINGS IRISH COFFEE

1 tbsp.	Irish whiskey	15 mL
1-2 tsp.	sugar	5-10 mL
2-4 tsp.	dry instant coffee	10-20 mL
⅔ cup	boiling water	150 mL
	chilled whipped cream	

In prewarmed 7 oz. (200 mL) stemmed goblet or coffee mug combine whiskey and sugar. Then combine instant coffee and boiling water. Fill goblet about ⅔ full with coffee, stirring until sugar is dissolved. Top with chilled whipped cream, letting it float on coffee.

HOT BUTTERED RUM I

1-2	sugar lumps	1-2
2 oz.	rum	60 mL
1 tsp.	butter	5 mL
4	cloves	4
	cinnamon stick	
	lemon slice	

In mug or old fashioned glass, dissolve sugar in a little hot water. Add rum, butter and cloves. Fill with boiling water and stir. Garnish with cinnamon stick and lemon slice.

HOT BUTTERED RUM II

2½ oz.	Navy or gold rum	75 mL
1	lemon slice	
1	cinnamon stick	
	cloves	
6-8 oz.	cider	175-250 mL
1 tbsp.	sweet butter	15 mL

Combine all, except the cider and butter, in a warmed mug. Add hot cider to the spiced rum. Top with butter and nutmeg.

HOT RUM TEA

1	mug hot tea	1
1 oz.	light or white rum	30 mL
	sugar to taste	
	cinnamon stick	

Combine, stir and serve.

HOT SPICED WASSAIL

6"	stick cinnamon, broken into pieces	15 cm
16	whole cloves	16
1 tsp.	whole allspice	5 mL
6 cups	apple juice or cider	1.5 L
2 cups	cranberry juice cocktail	500 mL
¼ cup	sugar	50 mL
1 tsp.	aromatic bitters	5 mL
3	medium oranges	3
	whole cloves to stud oranges	
1 cup	rum or to taste	250 mL
	orange slices	

In piece of cheesecloth wrap cinnamon, cloves and allspice. In large saucepan, combine juice or cider, cranberry juice, sugar and bitters. Add spice bag and studded oranges. Simmer, covered, 10 minutes. Add rum and heat through. Remove spices and oranges. Pour into warm serving bowl and float studded oranges and fresh orange slices on top.

Makes 9 cups (9 x 250 mL).

HOT TODDY

1½ oz.	rum, brandy or whiskey	45 mL
1 tsp.	sugar	5 mL
2	cloves	2
	lemon slice	

Put into a mug, add boiling water and cinnamon stick.

HOT WINE

3 cups	Sangria or white wine	750 mL
3 cups	dry red wine	750 mL
3 cups	water	750 mL
¼ tsp.	each of cinnamon, allspice and nutmeg	1 mL
4	whole cloves	4
¼ cup	white sugar	50 mL

Use 10-cup (2.5 L) coffee urn or pot, simmer to medium temperature and hold for 15 minutes.
Serve in hot toddy glass with cinnamon stick.

HOT ZOMBIE

1 oz.	each orange and lemon juice	30 mL
few drops	grenadine	few drops
	hot tea	
2 oz.	gold rum	60 mL
1 oz.	dark rum	30 mL
1 oz.	orange Curaçao	30 mL
few drops	Pernod	few drops
1 oz.	151-proof rum	30 mL

Combine the fruit juices and grenadine; add a little tea and mix well. Add the first 2 rums, Curaçao, and Pernod. Heat the 151-proof rum in a ladle; ignite and infuse in the mug. Extinguish, stir well, and serve hot.

HUNGARIAN COFFEE

1 tbsp.	grated German sweet chocolate	15 mL
	hot coffee	
2 tbsp.	cognac or brandy	25 mL
1	cinnamon stick	1
	whipped cream	

In coffee cup melt chocolate in hot coffee, add cognac or brandy and cinnamon stick. Top with whipped cream. Garnish with chocolate curls.

IRISH COFFEE

1 tsp.	sugar	5 mL
1½ oz.	Irish whiskey	45 mL
5 oz.	steaming coffee	160 mL
	whipped heavy cream	

Warm stemmed goblets. Place sugar in the glass. Pour in whiskey, then coffee. Stir, top with whipped cream.
See photograph on page 64.

KAHLÚA MOCHA COFFEE

1¼ oz.	Kahlúa	45 mL
	equal parts hot	
	chocolate and coffee	
	whipped cream	
dash	Kahlúa	dash

Combine Kahlúa, hot chocolate and coffee. Top off with whipped cream and a dash of Kahlúa.
See photograph on page 64.

MEXICAN COFFEE

3 tbsp.	Kahlúa	45 mL
1	cinnamon stick	1
	hot coffee	
	whipped cream	
	grated chocolate	

Place Kahlúa and cinnamon in cup, fill with coffee. Top with whipped cream and grated chocolate.

MULLED WINE

½ cup	sugar	125 mL
1½ cups	boiling water	375 mL
2 tsp.	lemon juice	10 mL
10	whole cloves	10
1 stick	cinnamon	1
26 oz.	dry red wine	750 mL
dash	nutmeg	dash

In a large saucepan, dissolve sugar in boiling water. Add lemon juice, cloves and cinnamon. Simmer 15 minutes. Remove cloves and cinnamon, add wine. Heat until very hot but do not boil. Pour into heated mugs; sprinkle with nutmeg.
Serves 12.
See photograph page 64.

RASPBERRY SPICED TEA

10 oz.	pkg. frozen raspberries	284 mL
3 cups	strong tea	750 mL
2 cups	clear apple juice	500 mL
2 tbsp.	sugar	30 mL
1 cup	white rum	250 mL
6	cinnamon sticks	6
6 slices	lemon, each studded	6 slices
	with 2 whole cloves	

In a saucepan combine raspberries, tea, apple juice and sugar. Simmer for 5 minutes or until the raspberries are thawed. Strain mixture into a bowl. Stir in the rum. Ladle into heat-proof glasses or cups. Add cinnamon sticks and lemon to each serving. Serve at once.
Makes 6 servings.

SCOTTISH McTEA

1 mug	hot tea	1
1 oz.	Scotch	30 mL
1 tbsp.	honey	15 mL

Combine, stir and serve while hot.

SKAHA SPECIAL

1 oz.	Kahlúa	30 mL
1 oz.	crème de menthe	30 mL
	hot chocolate	
	hot coffee	
	sweet whipped cream	
⅓ oz.	crème de menthe	10 mL
	shaved chocolate	

Combine Kahlúa and crème de menthe in a sugar-frosted goblet. Add equal parts hot chocolate and coffee, top with whipped cream, crème de menthe and chocolate.

SKIER'S SMOOTHIE

1 mug	hot tea	
1 oz.	Galliano	30 mL
	orange or lemon slice	

Combine tea and Galliano; add fruit slice garnish.

SPANISH COFFEE

⅓ oz.	Triple Sec	10 mL
⅓ oz.	brandy	10 mL
⅓ oz.	Kahlúa	10 mL
	hot coffee	
	sweet whipped cream	
⅓ oz.	Grand Marnier	10 mL

Combine first 3 ingredients in a sugar-frosted goblet. Fill with coffee, top with whipped cream and Grand Marnier.

SPICED CIDER PUNCH

2 x 4''	pieces stick cinnamon	2 x 10 cm
6	whole cloves	6
4	whole allspice	4
	thin peel from 1 orange (no white)	
	thin peel from 1 lemon (no white)	
⅓ cup	firmly packed light brown sugar	75 mL
8 cups	apple cider	2 L
1 cup	vodka	250 mL
½ cup	applejack (apple brandy)	125 mL

Tie cinnamon sticks, cloves, allspice and orange and lemon peels in cheesecloth. Combine with brown sugar and apple cider in a saucepan. Heat slowly, stirring until mixture just comes to a boil, but do not boil. Remove spice bag.

Carefully pour into a heat-proof punch bowl. Stir in vodka and apple brandy. Garnish with orange and lemon slices. Serve in warmed heat-proof punch cups or mugs with cinnamon sticks as stirrers.

Makes 20, 4 oz. (125 mL) servings.

SPICED TEA TODDY

4 cups	boiling water	1 L
8	tea bags	8
4 cups	apple juice	1 L
1 cup	port wine	250 mL
4	cloves	4
2	cinnamon sticks	2
½ cup	brown sugar	125 mL
	orange wedges	

Pour boiling water over tea. Cover and let steep 5 minutes. Remove tea bags. Meanwhile combine apple juice, port wine, 4 cloves, 2 cinnamon sticks and brown sugar in saucepan; simmer 5 minutes. Combine with tea. Serve in warm mugs. Garnish each mug with an orange wedge that has a whole clove stuck in the skin. Use a cinnamon stick as a stirrer.

Makes 8 cups (2 L).

SUNSHINE TEA

½ cup	sugar	125 mL
1½ cups	strong hot tea	375 mL
1 cup	orange juice	250 mL
¼ cup	lemon juice	50 mL
1 cup	light rum	250 mL
¼ cup	orange liqueur	50 mL
	orange and lemon slices	

Dissolve sugar in hot tea. Add remaining ingredients. Heat until steaming. Serve in warm mugs garnished with fruit slices. Makes 4 servings.

TOM AND JERRY I

1	egg, separated	1
1 tsp.	fine sugar	5 mL
1½ oz.	brandy	45 mL
1½ oz.	dark rum	45 mL
⅓ cup	hot milk	75 mL
	grated chocolate	

Beat egg white until stiff. Beat yolk until thick and lemon colored. Combine the white and yolk, beat in sugar. Add brandy, rum and milk. Serve in a warm glass topped with grated chocolate.

TOM AND JERRY II

2	eggs	2
2 tsp.	sugar	10 mL
pinch	baking soda	pinch
1½ oz.	brandy	45 mL
1½ oz.	rum	45 mL
	hot milk	

Separate eggs. Beat whites until frothy; add sugar and continue to beat until they form peaks. Beat yolks in a separate bowl until creamy. Combine yolks and whites and add baking soda. Divide egg mixture between 2 mugs; add half the brandy and rum to each. Fill mugs with hot milk.

TURKISH COFFEE

1 cup	hot black coffee	250 mL
2 tsp.	cognac	10 mL
	sugar to taste	

Combine, stir well and serve while hot.

WINE TEA

½ mug	hot tea	
½ mug	hot wine	
	slice of lemon	
	sugar to taste	

Combine and serve.

WINTER SANGRIA

26 oz.	rosé wine	750 mL
1½ cups	pineapple juice	375 mL
1	orange, unpeeled, thinly sliced	1
10	whole allspice	10
4	whole cinnamon sticks	4
3 tbsp.	sugar	45 mL

In a large kettle, combine all ingredients, stirring to dissolve sugar. Heat to simmering point. Strain punch into serving pitcher. Float a few orange slices in pitcher, if desired. Serve hot.
Makes about 10, 4-oz. (125 mL) servings.

BACCIO

14 oz.	grapefruit juice	398 mL
13 oz.	gin	369 mL
13 oz.	anisette	369 mL
	sugar to taste	
26 oz.	sparkling wine	750 mL

Mix all except the wine in punch bowl, with an ice block. Add lots of fresh fruit and the sparkling wine.
Serves 6.

BUDDHA PUNCH

26 oz.	sparkling wine	750 mL
26 oz.	wine	750 mL
1 cup	orange juice	250 mL
1 cup	lemon juice	250 mL
½ cup	Curaçao or orange liqueur	125 mL
½ cup	golden rum	125 mL
26 oz.	soda water	750 mL
	few dashes of bitters	

Mix all except soda water in large punch bowl with ice block. Add soda water when ready to serve. Garnish with mint leaves and slices of fresh fruit.
Serves 10.

BURGUNDY PUNCH

2 x 26 oz.	burgundy wine	2 x 750 mL
16 oz.	port	500 mL
8 oz.	cherry brandy	250 mL
	juice of 3 lemons	
6	oranges	6
4 oz.	berry sugar	125 mL
2 x 26 oz.	soda water	2 x 750 mL

Mix all except soda water. Add it when ready to serve. Decorate with fruit.
Serves 12.

CHAMPAGNE DELIGHT PUNCH

	strawberry slices	
½ cup	maraschino cherries, halved	125 mL
13 oz.	each of cognac, maraschino cordial	369 mL
2 x 26 oz.	dry white wine	2 x 750 mL
6 oz.	grenadine	170 mL
2 x 26 oz.	champagne	2 x 750 mL
3 x 26 oz.	sparkling water	3 x 750 mL

Place a block of ice in punch bowl, add strawberries and cherries. Add liqueurs, wine, grenadine and stir. When ready to serve add champagne and sparkling water. Stir gently.

CHAMPAGNE PUNCH

6¼ oz.	can frozen tangerine or orange juice concentrated, thawed	178 mL
12½ oz.	can apricot nectar, chilled	355 mL
4 oz	superfine granulated sugar	125 mL
13 oz.	orange liqueur	369 mL
26 oz.	club soda, chilled	750 mL
26 oz.	dry white wine, chilled	750 mL
26 oz.	champagne, chilled	750 mL
	ice ring or block	
	canned apricot halves, optional	

Combine juices, sugar and liqueur in a large chilled punch bowl.

Stir to dissolve sugar.

Stir in club soda, wine and champagne. Float ice ring on top. Serve in punch cups or champagne glasses. Add an apricot half to each, if desired.

Makes 26, 4-oz. (125 mL) servings.

This recipe can be made ahead of time by leaving out club soda and spirits until just before serving.

1. Frosty Lime Punch, page 100
2. Sunburst Punch, page 107
3. Cranberry Wine Punch, page 81
4. Beer, page 47

CRANBERRY WINE PUNCH

10 oz.	frozen strawberries	284 mL
1 cup	superfine sugar	250 mL
½ cup	brandy	125 mL
48 oz.	cranberry juice	1.36 L
26 oz.	club soda	750 mL
26 oz.	sparkling wine	750 mL

Whirl first 3 ingredients in blender until smooth. (Can be made ahead and chilled at this point.) Pour into chilled punch bowl. Stir in chilled cranberry juice cocktail, chilled club soda and chilled sparkling white wine. Float ice ring. Serve in punch cups with cranberries and strawberries on decorative picks.
See photograph page 80.

FRENCH "75" PITCHER

4 oz.	brandy	125 mL
2-3 dashes	bitters	2-3
	twists of lemon peel	
2 x 26 oz.	sparkling wine (not dry)	2 x 750 mL

Fill pitcher with ice, add brandy and bitters. Twist peel over the ice. Stir, add chilled wine when ready to serve. Do not stir. Garnish with orange.
Makes 10, 3 oz. (45 mL) servings.

HAWAIIAN PUNCH

3	large pineapples	3
3 cups	powdered sugar	750 mL
16 oz.	rum	500 mL
16 oz.	brandy	500 mL
16 oz.	lemon juice	500 mL
4 oz.	Curaçao	125 mL
4 oz.	maraschino liqueur	125 mL
4 x 26 oz.	champagne	4 x 750 mL

Crush pineapple pulp and combine with powdered sugar in a bowl. Leave for a few hours. Place in a large punch bowl; add all but the champagne. Stir well, let stand overnight. Add champagne and ice just before serving.

HOLIDAY EGGNOG

12	egg whites	12
½ cup	sugar	125 mL
12	egg yolks	12
1 cup	sugar	250 mL
¼ tsp.	salt	1 mL
4 cups	whipping cream, whipped	1 L
4 cups	milk	1 L
4 cups	whiskey	1 L
1 cup	rum	250 mL
	nutmeg	

Beat egg whites until stiff. Beat in the ½ cup (125 mL) sugar. Beat together the egg yolks, the 1 cup (250 mL) sugar and salt until very light. Combine egg mixtures and stir until thoroughly blended. Add whipped cream, milk and whiskey. Beat well. Add rum. Pour into quart (1 L) jars and store in cool place such as the refrigerator for 1 week to mellow. Shake or stir thoroughly. Before serving sprinkle each serving with nutmeg. Serves 30.

MERCEDES PUNCH

2 cups	grape juice	500 mL
½ lb.	sugar	250 mL
2 cups	dry red wine	500 mL
1 cup	Benedictine or similar liqueur	250 mL
2 cups	soda water	500 mL

Mix and serve over ice block.

MILK PUNCH

	cracked ice	
3 oz.	your choice liquor	45 mL
1 cup	milk	250 mL

Combine in shaker and shake well. Serve with sprinkle of nutmeg.

MIDORI MELONBALL PUNCH

26 oz.	Midori melon liqueur	750 mL
8 cups	orange, pineapple or grapefruit juice	2 L
12 oz.	vodka	375 mL
4 cups	club soda	1 L

Pour all ingredients over a large block of ice in a large punch bowl. Add club soda just before serving. Garnish punch bowl with fresh or frozen melonballs.

NECTAR PUNCH

2 x 48 oz.	cans apple juice	2 x 1.36 L
48 oz.	can apricot nectar	1.36 L
48 oz.	can unsweetened grapefruit juice	1.36 L
¼ cup	lemon juice	50 mL
1 cup	spice syrup (below)	250 mL
1 cup	strong tea	250 mL
15 cups	ice water	3.75 L
2 x 26 oz.	gin or vodka	2 x 750 mL
¾ cup	vermouth, sweet or dry	175 mL
3 x 26 oz.	ginger ale	3 x 750 mL

Combine fruit juices, spice syrup, tea and ice water. Chill. Just before serving, add gin or vodka and vermouth and pour into punch bowl over large piece of ice. Add ginger ale slowly; to keep the sparkle avoid stirring.

Makes about 120-4 oz. (125 mL) servings.

SPICE SYRUP

1½ cups	water	375 mL
½ cup	sugar	125 mL
½	stick cinnamon	½
5-6	whole cloves	5-6

Combine all ingredients, bring to boil and simmer 5 minutes. Cool and strain before using.

Makes 2 cups (500 mL).

ORANGE-LIME PUNCH

3½ cups	orange juice	875 mL
3 tsp.	lime juice	15 mL
½ cup	crushed ice	50 mL
6	maraschino cherries	6
¼ cup	sugar	50 mL
6 oz.	vodka or gin	175 mL
26 oz.	ginger ale	750 mL

Place orange juice, lime juice, crushed ice, maraschino cherries and sugar in punch bowl with ice and chill. When ready to serve, add vodka or gin and ginger ale and serve immediately. More ginger ale may be added, if desired. Garnish with lime.

PEACH PUNCH

2 x 10 oz.	pkg. frozen peaches	2 x 284 mL
1 cup	brandy	250 mL
26-35 oz.	sauterne	750-1 L
2 x 26 oz.	champagne	2 x 750 mL

Place together first 3 ingredients and chill. Add orange slices for decoration. When ready to serve, add chilled champagne.

PINA COLADA PUNCH

16 oz.	can coconut milk or cream	500 mL
2 tbsp.	lemon juice	30 mL
2 cups	golden or light rum	500 mL
48 oz.	can pineapple juice, chilled	1.36 L
	crushed ice	
2 x 19 oz.	cans pineapple chunks	2 x 540 mL
	maraschino cherries with stems	

Combine coconut milk and lemon juice in container of electric blender. Cover, whirl 30 seconds or until smooth. Pour into large chilled pitcher.

Stir in rum and pineapple juice. Pour over crushed ice in punch cups or glasses. Garnish with pineapple chunks and maraschino cherries.

To make-ahead. 1 or 2 hours ahead, prepare punch and refrigerate. Fill punch cups ¼ full with crushed ice. Tuck in a pineapple chunk. Place ice-filled punch cups on tray in freezer. Pull out when ready to serve. Pour punch over ice. Keep additional crushed ice in freezer.

Makes 18, 4-oz. (125 mL) servings.

PLANTER'S PUNCH

3 oz.	Jamaican rum	90 mL
1 oz.	lemon or lime juice	30 mL
1 tsp.	sugar	5 mL
	OR	
1 oz.	sugar syrup	30 mL
1 oz.	orange juice	30 mL
few drops	grenadine	few drops

Combine with ice. Shake well. Strain onto crushed ice. Garnish with a cherry, lemon or oragne. Serve in Collins glass.

RUM PUNCH I

16 oz.	cranberry juice cocktail	500 mL
16 oz.	cider or apple juice	500 mL
16 oz.	gold rum	500 mL
32 oz.	ginger ale, chilled	1 L
	lemon and lime slices	

Mix juices and rum in a large container. Refrigerate until party time. To serve place chilled mixture in a large punch bowl. Stir in chilled ginger ale. Garnish with lemon and lime slices.

RUM PUNCH II

4 cups	cold strong tea	1 L
	vanilla beans	
26 oz.	Jamaican rum	750 mL
8 oz.	lime juice	250 mL

Make ice from tea. Steep a few vanilla beans in the bottle of rum for several hours, then combine the rum with remaining ingredients in a large punch bowl and stir. Add ice before serving.

STRAWBERRY PUNCH

32 oz.	strawberries	1 L
1¼ cups	sugar	300 mL
⅓ cup	lemon juice	75 mL
16 oz.	ginger ale	500 mL
2 x 26 oz.	dry white wine	2 x 750 mL

Put strawberries in a bowl with sugar and lemon juice and chill for several hours. When ready to serve, put berries in punch bowl and add the remaining liquids and ice.

SYLLABUB

1 cup	sugar	250 mL
3 cups	white wine	750 mL
	juice of ¼ lemon	
3 tbsp.	grated lemon rind	45 mL
1 tsp.	light corn syrup	5 mL
½ tsp.	aromatic bitters	2 mL
2	egg whites	2
¼ cup	sugar	50 mL
2 cups	milk	500 mL
1 cup	light cream	250 mL

In large bowl, combine 1 cup (250 mL) sugar, wine, lemon juice, lemon rind, corn syrup and bitters. Stir until sugar dissolves. Chill several hours. Just before serving beat egg whites until foamy-white. Beat in ¼ cup (50 mL) sugar, 1 tbsp. (15 mL) at a time, until meringue stands in stiff peaks. Beat milk and cream into wine mixture until frothy; pour into punch bowl. Spoon meringue in small puffs on top. Serve in punch bowl. Float meringue on each serving.

Makes 13 punch-cup servings.

24-HOUR COCKTAIL

12	lemons	12
12	oranges	12
8 oz.	sugar	250 mL
1 quart	whiskey	1 L
16 oz.	pinapple juice	500 mL
	cherries	

Slice lemons, saving the rinds. Squeeze the juice into a crock pot; add the sugar, whiskey and a pint of boiling water. Drop in the rinds. Close the crock and store overnight. The next afternoon, strain, squeeze in the juice of the oranges, and pour over chunk of ice. Garnish with cherries.

VELVET

26 oz.	Moselle Wine	750 mL
1 cup	sherry	250 mL
2 tbsp.	powdered sugar	30 mL
1	lemon	1

Mix first 3 ingredients. Peel lemon very thinly and add just enough to flavor. Strain ingredients into a large punch bowl. Add ice and decorate with fruit.

ZIPPY EGGNOG

8 cups	ready-made, chilled eggnog	2 L
½ cup	orange juice, chilled orange, grated rind of 1 orange	125 mL
2 cups	whipped cream	500 mL
2 cups	rum	500 mL

Mix eggnog with orange juice and rind in punch bowl. Fold in whipped cream and keep chilled. Add rum, and a slice of orange for decoration. Serve immediately.

BITTER-SWEET COCKTAIL

¼ cup	strong tea	50 mL
2 tbsp.	orange juice	30 mL
dash	Angostura bitters	dash

Shake with crushed ice. Strain into small cocktail glass. Garnish with cocktail cherry and a lemon twist.
See photograph page 16.

CAESAR I

	celery salt	
1 dash	Tabasco	1 dash
2 dashes	Worcestershire sauce	2 dashes
	salt and pepper to taste	
	Clamato juice	
	celery stick	
	lime slice	

Rim glass with celery salt. Over ice cubes, add Tabasco, Worcestershire sauce, salt and pepper. Fill glass with Clamato juice. Garnish with celery and lime.

CAESAR II

1 cup	tomato juice	250 mL
2 tbsp.	lemon juice	30 mL
¾ tsp.	Worcestershire sauce	3 mL
½ tsp.	sugar	2 mL
dash	each Tabasco, celery salt, salt	dash
	grating of fresh pepper	

Combine and stir to blend. Pour over ice cubes in a large glass. Add celery stick as a muddler.

CASSIS LEMONADE

	juice of 1 lemon	
2 tbsp.	cassis syrup	30 mL

Combine in tall glass, add ice cubes. Fill with cold soda water.

CRANBERRY JUICE COCKTAIL

4 cups	cranberries	1 L
4 oz.	each of lemon, orange and pineapple juice	125 mL
8 oz.	sugar	250 mL

Boil the cranberries in 1 quart (1 L) of water until soft. Allow to cool. Strain the juice. Add the sugar and stir until it has dissolved. Add the fruit juices plus chunks of ice when ready to serve.

CRANBERRY KISS

1	sugar cube	1
½ cup	chilled sugar-free cranberry juice cocktail	125 mL
3 drops	aromatic bitters	3

Place sugar cube in shallow champagne glass. Add cranberry juice and bitters. Let stand a few minutes until sugar dissolves. Garnish with frozen cranberry.

CRANBERRY WASSAIL

¼ tsp.	ground nutmeg, cinnamon and allspice	1 mL
2 oz.	orange pekoe tea	60 mL
1 cup	sugar	250 mL
8 oz.	orange juice	250 mL
4 oz.	lemon juice	125 mL
2 oz.	cranberry juice	60 mL

Combine the spices and tea in a cloth sack. Infuse it in 2 quarts (2 L) of boiling water. Immediately remove from heat; allow to steep for 15 minutes. Strain. Add sugar and juices; reheat and stir until sugar has dissolved. Serve piping hot.

FRAMBOISE LEMONADE

	juice 1 lemon	
2 tbsp.	framboise syrup	30 mL

Combine in tall glass. Add 4 ice cubes. Fill with cold soda water.
Framboise syrup is raspberry syrup.
See photograph page 16.

GINGERY TEA

48 oz.	can unsweetened orange or pineapple juice	1.36 L
¼ cup	brown sugar	50 mL
2	cinnamon sticks	2
2″	piece fresh ginger root, peeled and sliced	5 cm
1½ cups	strong hot tea orange or lemon slices	375 mL

Combine juice, brown sugar, cinnamon sticks and ginger in saucepan. Simmer 5 minutes to blend flavors. Add tea and heat to steaming. Remove cinnamon and ginger. Serve in warm mugs, garnished with orange or lemon slices.
Makes 4½ cups (1 L).

HONEYDEW MELON COOLER

1 cup	chilled, cut-up honeydew melon	250 mL
⅓ cup	chilled orange juice	75 mL
1 cup	crushed ice	250 mL
1 drop	green food coloring	1

In blender whirl melon chunks and orange juice until smooth. Add crushed ice and food coloring. Whirl only to blend, allowing some ice to remain in drink. Pour equal amounts into 2, 8-oz. (250 mL) glasses. If desired, garnish with a mint sprig and a honeydew melon ball on a skewer. Serve at once.

LIME COOLER

4½ oz.	lime juice	135 mL
6 oz.	orange juice	175 mL
2 tbsp.	lemon juice	30 mL
	mint sprigs, crushed	
	sugar	
16 oz.	club soda	500 mL

Combine the fruit juices with the crushed mint in a punch bowl, allow to stand at least 1 hour. Strain and add sugar to taste. Stir well until the sugar is dissolved. Add soda and chunks of ice before serving.

MANGO CHI CHI

1	mango, cut up	1
1½ cups	chilled strawberries	375 mL
1 tbsp.	chilled lime juice	15 mL
1½ cups	chilled sugar-free ginger ale	375 mL

In blender whirl mango chunks, strawberries and lime juice until smooth. Remove blender container. Tilt container; gradually pour ginger ale down side to avoid too much fizz. Pour equal amounts into 4, 8-oz. (250 mL) glasses. Garnish with a lime slice. Serve at once.

Makes 4, 6-oz. (175 mL) servings.

MELON CRÈMEDREME

½ cup	each frozen unsweetened cantaloupe and honeydew-melon balls	125 mL
	OR	
½ cup	each fresh cantaloupe and honeydew melon pieces, frozen	125 mL
1 cup	chilled, sugar-free lemon-lime soda	250 mL

In blender whirl melon balls or pieces until smooth. Add soda; blend just to mix. Pour equal amounts into 2, 8-oz. (250 mL) glasses. Serve at once.

MOCK CHAMPAGNE I

1	sugar cube	1
2 drops	aromatic bitters	2 drops
½ cup	chilled club soda or sugar-free tonic water	125 mL

Place sugar cube in center of a chilled champagne glass. Pour bitters on top; let stand until cube dissolves slightly. Add club soda to fill glass. Serve at once.
See photograph page 16.

MOCK CHAMPAGNE II

4 oz.	white grape juice	125 mL
4 oz.	grapefruit juice	125 mL
2 cups	club soda	500 mL
few drops	concentrated lime juice Angostura bitters	few drops

Chill all the ingredients extremely well. Combine the juices; stir well, and before serving add the soda. Stir gently. Touch each serving up with a dash or 2 of bitters.

MOONLIGHT COCKTAIL

¾ cup	canned or fresh grapefruit juice	175 mL
½ tsp.	grenadine	2 mL
	crushed ice	
	lime slice	

Shake grapefruit juice with grenadine and crushed ice. Pour into old fashioned glass. Add short straws, and garnish with a slice of lime on side of glass.

ORANGE TONIC

¼ cup	crushed ice	50 mL
⅓ cup	chilled orange juice	75 mL
⅓ cup	chilled, sugar-free tonic water	75 mL
1 dash	orange bitters	1 dash
	orange slice for garnish	

Place crushed ice in 10 oz. (285 mL) glass, add orange juice, tonic water and bitters; stir. Garnish with orange slice. Serve with colored straw.

SHIRLEY TEMPLE

ginger ale
grenadine
cherries

Fill a champagne glass with ginger ale and add several drops of grenadine; stir gently and decorate with a couple of cherries. See photograph page 16.

SPICED TEA TODDY

4 cups	boiling water	1 L
8	tea bags	8
4 cups	apple juice	1 L
4	cloves	4
2	cinnamon sticks	2
½ cup	brown sugar	125 mL

Pour boiling water over tea bags. Cover and let steep 5 minutes. Remove tea bags. Meanwhile, combine remaining ingredients and simmer 5 minutes. Combine with tea. Serve in warm mugs. Garnish each mug with an orange wedge that has a whole clove stuck in the skin. Use a cinnamon stick as a stirrer.

Makes 8 cups (2 L).

TOM AND JERRY

1	egg	1
2 tbsp.	confectioner's suger	30 mL
1 tsp.	instant coffee	5 mL
½ tsp.	vanilla	2 mL
½ tsp.	brandy extract	2 mL
¼ tsp.	rum extract	1 mL
¼ tsp.	cinnamon	1 mL
⅛ tsp.	allspice	0.5 mL
⅛ tsp.	cloves	0.5 mL
⅓ cup	nonfat dry milk powder	75 mL
2 cups	boiling water	500 mL

In bowl, beat egg and sugar until fluffy. Blend in coffee, extracts and spices. In medium bowl, stir water into milk powder; stir in egg mixture.

Serves 4 (55 calories)

TONIC COOLER

	fresh lemon rind	
6 dashes	of bitters	6 dashes
	lemon slice	
	cracked ice	
	tonic water	

Twist lemon rind to let oil spray inside the glass. Add bitters, lemon slice and cracked ice. Fill the glass with tonic water. Serve with straws.

ALMOND CRANBERRY PUNCH

6 cups	chilled cranberry juice cocktail	1.5 L
½ cup	chilled bottled lime juice	125 mL
2 cups	chilled pineapple juice	500 mL
¼-½ cup	sugar	50-125 mL
½ tsp.	almond extract	2 mL
2 x 26 oz.	ginger ale	2 x 750 mL
	ice block or mold	

Put first 5 ingredients in punch bowl. Stir until sugar is dissolved; add ginger ale, stirring very gently. Add ice block or mold.

ANGEL PUNCH

8 cups	white grape juice	2 L
4 cups	green tea	1 L
2 cups	lemon juice	500 mL
8 oz.	sugar syrup	250 mL
2 x 26 oz.	club soda	2 x 750 mL

Combine everything except the soda; stir well and refrigerate several hours. Serve in ice with chilled soda.

APPLE CIDER PUNCH

1 gallon	apple cider	4 L
2 3" sticks	cinnamon	2
⅔ cup	sugar	150 mL
2	oranges	2
	whole cloves	
3 medium	apples	3

Heat cider, cinnamon, sugar to boiling point. Cover and simmer over low heat 20 minutes. Stud oranges with whole cloves. Strain punch and pour into bowl. Rinse glass punch bowl with warm water to heat before pouring in hot punch. Float oranges, red apples in punch bowl.

APRICOT PUNCH

12 oz.	can apricot nectar	341 mL
12 oz.	can unsweetened pineapple juice	341 mL
6¼ oz.	can frozen orange juice	178 mL
6¼ oz.	can lemonade	178 mL
1 tsp.	non-alcoholic apricot cordial	5 mL
26 oz.	carbonated water	750 mL
10-12 oz.	ginger ale	284-341 mL

Mix all ingredients except carbonated water and ginger ale in punch bowl. Stir well, add carbonated water and ginger ale just before serving.

CHERRY PUNCH

6 oz.	pkg. cherry gelatin	175 mL
2 cups	boiling water	500 mL
8 cups	chilled apple juice	2 L
½ cup	chilled lemon juice	125 mL
6 cups	lemon soda	1.5 L
	cracked ice	

Dissolve gelatin in water. Stir in fruit juices and mix well. Add soda. Chill with ice in punch bowl.
Makes about 3½ quarts (3.5L).

CHRISTMAS CRANBERRY PUNCH

2 cups	cranberry cocktail juice	500 mL
2 x 6½ oz.	cans frozen lemonade concentrate	2
4 cups	cold water	1 L
4 cups	ginger ale	1 L

Combine all ingredients except ginger ale, in punch bowl and mix well. Gently add ginger ale and ice before serving.

CHRISTMAS EGGNOG

6 cups	cold milk	1.5 L
6	eggs	6
¼ cup	sugar	50 mL
3 tsp.	vanilla	15 mL
6 scoops	ice cream	6 scoops
	nutmeg	

Put all ingredients together in a mixing bowl or blender; mix until smooth. Store in refrigerator until time to serve. Pour into punch cups. Sprinkle with nutmeg.
12 servings

COFFEE PUNCH

2 cups	vanilla ice cream, frozen hard	500 mL
2 cups	chocolate ice cream frozen hard	500 mL
1 tsp.	crème de cacao non-alcoholic syrup	5 mL
5 cups	hot coffee	1.25 L

Pour coffee over ice cream and beat lightly until partially melted. Add 1 tsp. (5 mL) of crème de cacao. Pour into punch glasses; sprinkle with nutmeg.

FESTIVAL CRANBERRY EGGNOG PUNCH

4 cups	eggnog	1 L
2 cups	chilled cranberry juice cocktail	500 mL
½ tsp.	salt	2 mL
1 tbsp.	lemon juice	15 mL
	red food colouring	

Combine eggnog, cranberry juice cocktail, salt and lemon juice until well blended. Add a few drops red food coloring to give delicate pink color. Serve well chilled.
Makes 6-8 glasses.

FESTIVE EGGNOG PUNCH

4 cups	ice cream, any flavor	1 L
8 cups	eggnog	2 L
	nutmeg	

Reserve 3-4 scoops of your favorite flavor ice cream for garnish. Soften remainder and beat into eggnog, chill thoroughly. Turn into punch bowl and float reserved ice cream on top. Sprinkle each serving with nutmeg.
Makes 10-12 servings.

FESTIVE ORANGE PUNCH

2 cups	vanilla ice cream	500 mL
1 cup	milk	250 mL
4 cups	eggnog	1 L
6¼ oz.	frozen orange juice concentrate, defrosted	178 mL

Soften ice cream, then blend smooth with milk. Combine all ingredients and serve chilled.
8 servings.

FROSTY LIME PUNCH

12½ oz.	can frozen lime juice	355 mL
12½ oz.	can frozen lemonade	355 mL
4	cans water	4 x 355 mL
2 cups	lime sherbet	500 mL
2 cups	ginger ale	500 mL
2 tsp.	bottled lime juice	10 mL
15-20	ice cubes	15-20

Combine all ingredients except ice in punch bowl and mix well. Just before serving, add the ice cubes. Serve in punch cups. Garnish with fresh mint, lemon or a red cherry.
Serves 12.
See photograph page 80.

FRUIT PARTY PUNCH

6¼ oz.	can frozen orange juice concentrate	178 mL
6¼ oz.	can frozen lemonade concentrate	178 mL
3 cups	pineapple juice	750 mL
6 cups	cranberry juice	1.5 L
	ice cubes	

Add water to orange juice and lemonade according to directions. Mix with other liquids and ice.

GOLDEN PUNCH I

2 cups	lemon juice, chilled	500 mL
2 cups	orange juice, chilled	500 mL
2 cups	sugar	500 mL
2 cups	cold water	500 mL
4 x 26 oz.	ginger ale, chilled	4 x 750 mL
	lemon slices	

Combine fruit juices, sugar and water in large punch bowl. Stir until sugar dissolves. Just before serving, pour ginger ale down side of bowl; stir gently. Float iced fruit garland in bowl. Garnish with mint leaves. Serve with cracked ice.
Makes about 40, ½ cup (125 mL) servings.

GOLDEN PUNCH II

2 cups	sugar	500 mL
12½ oz.	orange juice	355 mL
12½ oz.	lemon juice	355 mL
4 oz.	pineapple juice	125 mL
26 oz.	ginger ale	750 mL

Boil the sugar in 1 cup (250 mL) of water for several minutes, allow to cool. In a large punch bowl, combine the fruit juices with the cool sugar syrup and another 3 cups (750 mL) of water; stir well. Add the ginger ale plus ice before serving.

GOOD LUCK PUNCH

6 cups	cut-up rhubarb	1.5 L
	cold water	
3 cups	sugar	750 mL
2 cups	water	500 mL
	juice of 6 lemons	
1 cup	pineapple juice	250 mL
26 oz.	soda water	750 mL

Cut rhubarb in 1″ (2.5 cm) pieces. Add cold water to cover. Cook until very soft, about 10 minutes. Strain through a sieve lined with several thicknesses of cheesecloth. Discard rhubarb pulp. You should have about 8 cups (2 L) of rhubarb juice.

Combine sugar and 2 cups (500 mL) water in medium saucepan. Set over heat and stir until sugar is dissolved. Bring to a boil and boil hard 10 minutes. Cool. Pour rhubarb juice, sugar syrup, lemon juice and pineapple juice over a chunk of ice in a small punch bowl at serving time. Add soda water. Serve in punch cups.

Makes about 30 servings.

GRAPEFRUIT MINT PUNCH

1½ cups	sugar	375 mL
1 cup	cold water	250 mL
4 cups	orange juice	1 L
2 cups	lemon juice	500 mL
1 cup	grapefruit juice	250 mL
26 oz.	carbonated water	750 mL
	crushed fresh mint or	
	mint sprigs.	

Combine sugar and cold water in saucepan. Bring to boil, then simmer for 3 minutes. Add to mixture of other ingredients. Cool.
Serves 12.

GRAPEFRUIT PUNCH

2 x 12½ oz.	cans frozen grapefruit juice	2 x 355 mL
2 x 12½ oz.	cans pineapple juice	2 x 355 mL
6 x 12½ oz.	cans water	6 x 355 mL
2 x 26 oz.	ginger ale	2 x 750 mL

Pour all ingredients in punch bowl. Stir. Add ice cubes.

GRAPE PUNCH

12½ oz.	can frozen grape juice	355 mL
3 x 12½ oz.	cans water	3 x 355 mL
48 oz.	can pineapple juice	1.36 L
2 x 26 oz.	ginger ale	2 x 750 mL

Mix all ingredients. Put in punch bowl. Add block of ice.

HOLIDAY EGGNOG

6	eggs separated	6
½ cup	sugar	125 mL
2½ cups	milk	625 mL
¼ tsp.	salt	1 mL
2 cups	heavy cream whipped	500 mL
1 tbsp.	vanilla	15 mL
	nutmeg	

Beat egg yolks until light. Gradually add sugar, beating until thick and pale in color. Gradually add milk. Chill at least 3 hours. Fold in whipped cream, stiffly beaten egg whites and vanilla. Serve with sprinkled nutmeg.

Makes 16 servings.

HOT SPICY PUNCH

8 cups	cold water	2 L
¼ cup	peeled, chopped fresh ginger	50 mL
8	tea bags	8
4	sticks cinnamon, broken	4
6	whole cloves	6
8 cups	boiling water	2 L
½ cup	sugar	125 mL
1 cup	lemon juice	250 mL
1 cup	orange juice	250 mL
4 cups	pineapple juice	1 L
4 cups	cranberry juice cocktail	1 L
8 cups	apple juice	2 L
	thick orange slices	
	whole cloves	

Heat cold water in large kettle. Add ginger, bring to a boil, turn down heat, cover and simmer 15 minutes. Cool. Strain, return liquid to pan, discard ginger. Put tea bags, cinnamon and 6 cloves in a bowl. Add boiling water. Stir. Cover bowl and let tea steep 10 minutes. Strain into ginger water. Add all remaining ingredients except orange slices and cloves. Heat well and pour into punch bowl. Stick a clove in the rind of each orange slice and float on top of punch.

Makes about 60 servings.

LIME COOLER PUNCH

1 cup	bottled lime juice	250 mL
½ cup	granulated sugar	125 mL
	juice of 1 lime	
2 cups	lime sherbet	500 mL
2 cups	pineapple sherbet	500 mL
	lime slices	
	mint leaves	
2 x 26 oz.	sparkling water	2 x 750 mL

In a blender, combine lime juice and sugar. Blend until sugar is dissolved. Add 1 x 26 oz. of sparkling water and juice of 1 lime. Put all ingredients from blender into punch bowl and add the other bottle of sparkling water. Just before serving, add the lime and pineapple sherbet. Garnish with lime slices and mint leaves.

Makes 12 cups (3 L).

MINTED FRUIT PUNCH

1 cup	sugar	250 mL
4 cups	water	1 L
10 or more	fresh mint leaves	10
48 oz.	can pineapple juice	1.36 L
48 oz.	can orange juice	1.36 L
1 tsp.	nonalcoholic crème de menthe syrup	5 mL
½ cup	fresh lemon juice	125 mL
2 x 26 oz.	lemon-lime carbonated beverage	2 x 750 mL
	lemon and lime slices	

Bring sugar and water to boiling point. Pour over the mint leaves. Simmer for 10 minutes. Strain and chill. Place block of ice in large punch bowl. Over ice pour mint syrup, pineapple juice, orange juice, crème de menthe and lemon juice; stir to mix. Just before serving, add carbonated beverage. Stir lightly. Garnish with lemon and lime slices.

PINEAPPLE SHERBET PUNCH

6¼ oz.	frozen pink lemonade	178 mL
6¼ oz.	frozen orange juice	178 mL
4½ cups	carbonated water	1 L
2 cups	pineapple sherbet	500 mL
2 cups	vanilla ice cream	500 mL

Put fruit concentrates and water in punch bowl. Stir to blend. Fold in sherbet and ice cream. Serve at once.
Serves 10-12.

PINK LEMONADE PUNCH

2 x 12½ oz.	frozen pink lemonade	2 x 355 mL
8 x 12½ oz.	cans water	8 x 355 mL
2 x 26 oz.	ginger ale	2 x 750 mL

Mix all ingredients in punch bowl. Garnish with mint leaves, lime slices and ice cubes.

ROSY-RED PUNCH

48 oz.	can apple juice	1.36 L
3 cups	cranberry juice cocktail	750 mL
1½ cups	orange juice	375 mL
26 oz.	ginger ale	750 mL

Chill all ingredients. At serving time, combine juices in punch bowl. Garnish with slices of orange or decorative ice cubes. Add ginger ale slowly to keep the sparkle, avoid stirring.
Makes 25, 4 oz. (125 mL) servings.

SPARKLING ALE PUNCH

4 cups	cranberry juice	1 L
1 cup	sugar	250 mL
2 cups	orange juice	500 mL
1 cup	pineapple juice	250 mL
¾ cup	lemon juice	175 mL
2 cups	chilled ginger ale	500 mL
2 cups	pineapple sherbet	500 mL
2 cups	lemon sherbet	500 mL

Blend cranberry juice, sugar and fruit juices. Refrigerate until serving time. Just before serving, stir in ginger ale and sherbets. Serves 10-12.

SPARKLING RED PUNCH

6 cups	chilled cranberry cocktail juice	1.5 L
48 oz.	can pineapple juice chilled	1.36 L
26 oz.	chilled ginger ale	750 mL
1½ cups	pomegranate grenadine syrup	375 mL

Mix all ingredients in punch bowl. Make ice ring with fresh whole strawberries in mold.
Serves 25.

STRAWBERRY CREAM PUNCH

48 oz.	can pineapple juice, chilled	1.36 mL
¾ cup	sugar	175 mL
6¼ oz.	frozen pink lemonade	178 mL
2¼ cups	water	550 mL
4 cups	strawberry ice cream	1 L
2½ x 26 oz.	ginger ale	2½ x 750 mL

In punch bowl, combine pineapple juice, sugar lemonade concentrate and water. Add ice cream; stir until blended. Stir in ginger ale. Serve at once.

STRAWBERRY-PINEAPPLE PUNCH

6¼ oz.	frozen lemonade	178 mL
8 oz.	can crushed pineapple	250 mL
10 oz.	pkg. frozen strawberries	284 mL
1 tbsp.	pomegranate grenadine syrup	15 mL
3 x 26 oz.	ginger ale, chilled crushed ice	3 x 750 mL

Put lemonade concentrate, pineapple, strawberries and grenadine syrup in blender. Blend until completely smooth. Combine with ginger ale and pour over crushed ice in punch bowl.

SUNBURST PUNCH

2½ cups	orange juice	625 mL
2¼ cups	lemon juice	550 mL
2 cups	grenadine syrup	500 mL
2-3 x 26 oz.	ginger ale	2-3 x 750 mL

Mix juices well and pour over ice cubes in punch bowl. When ready to serve, add 2-3 bottles ginger ale. Punch may be decorated with fresh fruits: orange slices, fresh strawberries. See photograph page 80.

INDEX

INDEX

LIQUEURS

HOT DRINKS

INDEX

A Gift For Favored Friends
Garfield's Party Time Favorites

Please send _____ copies of **Garfield's Party Time Favorites** at $8.95 each, plus $1.50 (total orders) for postage and handling to:

NAME ....

STREET...

CITY ....

PROVINCE/STATE.........................POSTAL/ZIP CODE ....

Please make cheques or money orders payable to:

Garfield's Party Time Favorites Publishing
Site #35-6, R.R.#1
Okanagan Falls, British Columbia
Canada   V0H 1R0

A Gift For Favored Friends
Garfield's Party Time Favorites

Please send _____ copies of **Garfield's Party Time Favorites** at $8.95 each, plus $1.50 (total orders) for postage and handling to:

NAME ....

STREET...

CITY ....

PROVINCE/STATE.........................POSTAL/ZIP CODE ....

Please make cheques or money orders payable to:

Garfield's Party Time Favorites Publishing
Site #35-6, R.R.#1
Okanagan Falls, British Columbia
Canada   V0H 1R0